Culture in a Liquid Modern World

Zygmunt Bauman

Translated (from Polish) by Lydia Bauman

polity

in association with the
National Audiovisual Institute

First published in 2011 by Polity Press
Reprinted 2011

Polity Press
65 Bridge Street
Cambridge CB2 1UR, UK

Polity Press
350 Main Street
Malden, MA 02148, USA

ISBN-13: 978-0-7456-5354-9 (hb)
ISBN-13: 978-0-7456-5355-6 (pb)

A catalogue record for this book is available from the British Library.

Typeset in 11 on 14 pt Sabon
by Servis Filmsetting Ltd, Stockport, Cheshire
Printed and bound by MPG Books Group, UK

For further information on Polity, visit our website: www.politybooks.com

This book was commissioned by the National Audiovisual Institute for the European Culture Congress, 8–11 September 2011, Wrocław, Poland.

www.nina.gov.pl

www.culturecongress.eu

Contents

I

Some notes on the historical peregrinations of the concept of 'Culture'

On the basis of findings made in Great Britain, Chile, Hungary, Israel and Holland, a thirteen-strong team led by the highly respected Oxford sociologist John Goldthorpe concluded that a cultural elite can no longer be readily distinguished from those lower in the cultural hierarchy by the old signs: regular attendance at the opera and concerts, an enthusiasm for everything regarded as 'high art' at any given moment, and a habit of turning up its nose at 'all that is common, like a pop song, or mainstream television'. Which is not at all to say that one does not still come across those who are regarded, not least by themselves, as the cultural elite, true art lovers, people better informed than their not quite so cultured peers as to what culture is about, what it consists of and what is deemed *Comme il faut* or *comme il ne faut pas* – what is suitable or not suitable – for a man or woman of culture. Except that, unlike those latter-day cultural elites, they are not 'connoisseurs' in the strict sense of the word, looking down on the taste of the common man, or the tastelessness of the philistine. Rather, it is more appropriate today to describe them – using the term coined by Richard A Petersen, of Vanderbilt University – as 'omnivorous': there is room in their repertory of cultural consumption for both opera and heavy metal or punk, for 'high art' and mainstream television, for Samuel Beckett and Terry Pratchett. A bite of this, a morsel of that, this today, tomorrow something else. A mixture . . . according to Stephen Fry, authority on modish trends and shining light of the most exclusive London society (as well as star of some of the most popular TV shows). He publicly admits:

> Well, people can be dippy about all things digital and still read books, they can go to the opera and watch a cricket match and apply for Led Zeppelin tickets without splitting themselves asunder. . . You like Thai food? But what is wrong with Italian? Woah, there. . . calm down. I like both. Yes. It can be done. I can like rugby football and the musicals of Stephen Sondheim. High Victorian Gothic and the installations of Damien Hirst. Herb Alpert's Tijuana Brass and piano works of Hindemith. English hymns and Richard Dawkins. First editions of Norman Douglas and iPods, snooker, darts, and ballet. . .

Or, as Petersen put it in 2005, summing up twenty years of inquiry: 'We see a shift in elite status group politics from those highbrows who snobbishly disdain all base, vulgar, or mass popular culture. . . to those highbrows who omnivorously consume a wide range of popular as well as highbrow art forms. . .'[1] In other words no works of culture are alien to me: I don't identify with any of them a hundred per cent, totally and absolutely, and certainly not at the price of denying myself other pleasures. I feel at home everywhere, despite the fact (or perhaps because of it) that there is no place I can call home. It isn't so much a confrontation of one (refined) taste against another (vulgar) one, but of omnivorousness against univorousness, a readiness to consume everything against finicky selectiveness. The cultural elite is alive and kicking; it is today more active and eager than ever before – but it is too preoccupied with tracking hits and other celebrated culture-related events to find time for formulating canons of faith, or converting others to them.

Apart from the principle of 'don't be fussy, don't be choosy' and 'consume more', it has nothing to say to the univorous throng at the bottom of the cultural hierarchy.

And yet, as Pierre Bourdieu maintained only a few decades ago, every artistic offering used to be addressed to a specific social class, and to that class alone – and was accepted only, or primarily by that class. The triple effect of those artistic offerings – class definition, class segregation and manifestation of class membership – was, according to Bourdieu, their essential raison d-être, the most important of their social functions, perhaps even their hidden, if not their professed aim.

According to Bourdieu, works of art intended for aesthetic consumption pointed out, signalled and protected class divisions, legibly marking and fortifying interclass boundaries. In order to unequivocally mark boundaries and to protect them effectively, all *objets d'art*, or at least a significant majority, had to be assigned to mutually exclusive sets; sets whose contents were not to be mixed, or approved of or possessed simultaneously.

What counted were not so much their contents or innate qualities as their differences, their mutual intolerance and a ban on their conciliation, erroneously presented as a manifestation of their innate, immanent resistance to morganatic relationships. There were elite tastes, 'high culture' by nature, average or 'philistine' tastes typical of the middle class, and 'vulgar' tastes, worshipped by the lower class – and it was no easier to mix them with than fire and water. It may be that nature abhors a vacuum, but culture definitely does not tolerate a mélange. In Bourdieu's *Distinction*, culture manifested itself above all as a useful appliance, consciously intended to mark out class differences and to safeguard them: as a technology invented for the creation and protection of class divisions and social hierarchies.[2]

Culture, in short, manifested itself in a form similar to that described a century earlier by Oscar Wilde: 'Those who find beautiful meanings in beautiful things are the cultivated. . . They are the elect to whom beautiful things mean only Beauty.'[3] 'The elect', chosen ones, that is to say those who sing the glory of those values they themselves uphold, at one and the same time ensuring their own victory in the song contest. Inevitably they will find beautiful meanings in beauty, since it is they who decide what beauty is; even before the search for beauty began, who was it, if not the chosen ones, who decided where to look for that beauty (at the opera, not at the music hall or on the market stall; in galleries, not on city walls or in cheap prints gracing working-class or peasant homes; in leather-bound volumes, not in newsprint or cheap penny-publications). The chosen ones are chosen not by virtue of their insight into what is beautiful, but rather by the fact that the statement 'this is beautiful' is binding precisely because it was uttered by them and confirmed by their actions. . .

Sigmund Freud believed that aesthetic knowledge searches in vain for the essence, nature and sources of beauty, its so to speak immanent qualities – and tends to hide its ignorance in a stream of pompous and self-important, and ultimately empty pronouncements. 'Beauty has no obvious use', decrees Freud, 'nor is there any cultural necessity for it. Yet civilization could not do without it'.[4]

But, on the other hand, as Bourdieu implies, there are benefits from beauty and a need for it. Although the benefits are not 'disinterested', as Kant suggested, they are benefits nevertheless, and while the need is not necessarily cultural, it is social; and it is very likely that both the benefits from and the need for telling beauty from ugliness, or subtlety from vulgarity, will last as long as there exists a need and a desire to tell high society from low society, and the connoisseur of refined tastes from the tasteless, vulgar masses, plebs and riff-raff . . .

Upon careful consideration of these descriptions and interpretations, it becomes clear that 'culture' (a set of preferences suggested, recommended and imposed on account of their correctness, goodness or beauty) was regarded by its authors as first and foremost and in the final resort to be a 'socially conservative' force. In order to prove itself in this function, culture had to perform, with equal commitment, two apparently contradictory acts of subterfuge. It had to be as emphatic, severe and uncompromising in its endorsements as in its disapprovals, in its granting of entry tickets as its withholding of them, in its authorizing of identity papers as in its denial of citizens' rights. As well as identifying what was desirable and commendable by virtue of being 'how it should be' – familiar and cosy – culture needed signifiers for what was to be mistrusted and avoided on account of its baseness and hidden menace; signs warning, as on the rims of ancient maps, that *hic sunt leones*, here there be lions. Culture was to behave just like the castaway in the English parable, apparently ironic but moralizing in intent, who had to build three dwellings on the desert island where he had been shipwrecked in order to feel at home, that is to say, to acquire an identity and defend it effectively: the first dwelling was his private quarters, the second was the club he frequented every Saturday, and the third had the sole function of being the place whose threshold the castaway would assiduously avoid crossing in all the long years he would spend on the island.

On its publication over thirty years ago, Bourdieu's *Distinction* turned upside down the original concept of 'culture' born in the Enlightenment and then passed on from generation to generation. The meaning of culture as it was discovered, defined and documented by Bourdieu was remote from the concept of 'culture' hammered out and introduced into common parlance in the third quarter of the eighteenth century, almost simultaneously with the English concept of 'refinement' and the German *Bildung*.

According to its original concept, 'culture' was to be an agent for change rather than for preservation of the status quo; or more precisely, it was to be a navigation tool to steer social evolution towards a universal human condition. The initial purpose of the concept of 'culture' was not to serve as a register of descriptions, inventories and codifications of the prevailing situation, but rather to appoint a goal and direction for future efforts. The name of 'culture' was accorded to a proselytizing mission planned and undertaken in the form of attempts to educate the masses and refine their customs, and through these to improve society and advance 'the people', that is to say, those from the 'depths of society', to those on its heights. 'Culture' was associated with a 'beam of enlightenment' reaching 'under the eaves' of country and town dwellings and into the dark recesses of prejudice and superstition which, like so many vampires (it was believed), would not survive exposure to the light of day. According to the impassioned pronouncement by Matthew Arnold in his very influential and tellingly named book *Culture or Anarchy* (1869), 'culture' 'seeks to do away with classes; to make the best that has been thought or known in the world current everywhere; to make all men live in an atmosphere of sweetness and light'; and again, according to an opinion expressed by Arnold in his introduction to *Literature and Dogma* (1873), culture is the blending of human dreams and desires with the toil of those willing and able to satisfy them: 'Culture is the passion for sweetness and light, and (what is more) the passion of making them prevail.'

'Culture' entered the modern vocabulary as a declaration of intent; the name of a mission yet to be undertaken. The concept of culture alone was a catchword and a call to action. Like the concept which provided the metaphor to describe this intent (that is, the concept of 'agriculture', associating farmers with the fields they cultivated), it was a call to the ploughman and the sower to till and sow the barren land and enrich the harvest by cultivation (Cicero even used this metaphor, describing the upbringing of the young by

---

the term *cultura animi*). The concept assumed a division between the relatively few educators, called to cultivate souls, and those many who were to be the subject of cultivation; the guardians and the guarded, the supervisors and the supervised, the educators and the educated, the producers and their products, subjects and objects – and a meeting to take place between them.

'Culture' inferred a planned and expected agreement between those possessing knowledge (or at least confident of being in possession of it) and ignoramuses (or those thus described by the confident aspirants to their education); an agreement furnished, incidentally, with only one signature, unilaterally endorsed, and realized under the exclusive directorship of the newly formed 'educated class', seeking the right to fashion the 'new and improved' order rising from the ashes of the ancien régime. The declared intention of this class was the education, enlightenment, elevation and ennobling of *le peuple*, recent recipients of the role of *citoyens* of the newly formed *état-nation:* that pairing of a newly formed nation elevating itself to a sovereign state existence, with the new state aspiring to the role of a trustee, defender and guardian of that nation.

The 'enlightenment project' gave culture (understood as an activity akin to land cultivation) the status of a basic tool for the building of a nation, a state, and a nation-state – at the same time entrusting that tool to the hands of the educated class. In its perambulations between political ambitions and philosophical deliberations, a twin goal of the enlightenment undertaking had soon crystallized (whether openly announced or tacitly assumed) into the double postulate of the obedience of subjects and solidarity among fellow countrymen.

The growth in the 'populace' added self-confidence to the forming nation-state, since it was believed that increases in the numbers of potential worker-soldiers would augment its power and guarantee its security. However, because the joint effort of nation-building and economic growth also resulted in an increasing surplus of individuals (in essence, whole categories of the population needed to be confined to the scrapheap if the desired order was to be born and grow in strength, and wealth creation was to increase its momentum) the newly established nation-state soon faced an urgent need to search for new territory beyond its borders: territory capable of absorbing the excess of population which it was no longer able to accommodate within its own boundaries.

The prospect of colonization of farflung dominions proved a powerful stimulus to culture's enlightenment idea and gave the proselytizing mission an altogether new, potentially worldwide dimension. In a mirror image of the vision of the 'enlightenment of the people', a concept was shaped of the 'white man's mission' and of 'saving the savage from his barbaric state'. Soon these concepts were to be furnished with a theoretical commentary in the form of an evolutionary cultural theory which promoted the 'developed' world to the status of unquestionable perfection, to be imitated and aspired to sooner or later by the rest of the globe. In the pursuit of this goal, the rest of the world was to be actively helped and, in the event of resistance, coerced. The evolutionary cultural theory gave 'developed' society the function of converting the rest of the inhabitants of the globe.

All its future initiatives and undertakings were reduced to the role destined to be played out by the educated elite of the colonial metropolis before their own metropolitan 'populace'.

Bourdieu devised his research and collected and interpreted the data thus discovered at a time when the efforts above were beginning to lose their momentum and their sense of direction, and generally speaking were a spent force – at least within the metropolis, where the visions of the awaited and postulated future were being concocted, though less so on the peripheries of the empire, from which expeditionary forces were compelled to return long before they had succeeded in bringing the realities of the life of the native up to the standards espoused in the metropolis. As for the metropolis, the declaration of intent of two hundred years standing succeeded in establishing there a wide network of executive institutions, founded and administered mainly by the state – already sufficiently vigorous to be reliant upon its own momentum, entrenched routine and bureaucratic inertia. The intended product (a 'populace' turned into a 'civic body') was formed and the position of the educating classes in the new order was assured – or at least accepted as such. Rather than the daring, venturesome endeavour, crusade or mission of old, culture now likened itself to a homeostatic device: a kind of gyroscope protecting the nation-state from changing winds and cross-currents and helping it, despite tempests and the caprices of changing weather, to 'steer the ship on its right course' (or, as Talcott Parsons would have it in his then popular expression: to enable the 'system' to 'regain its own equilibrium').

In short, 'culture' was transformed from a stimulant into a tranquilizer; from the arsenal of a modern revolution into a repository of conservation products.

'Culture' became the name for functions ascribed to stabilizers, homeostats or gyroscopes. It was in the midst of these functions (short-lived, it was soon to turn out) that culture was captured and immobilized, registered and analysed, as in a snapshot, in Bourdieu's *Distinction*. Bourdieu's report did not escape the timing of Minerva's proverbial owl, that goddess of all knowledge: Bourdieu was observing a landscape illuminated by the setting sun, which momentarily sharpened contours which were soon to dissolve in the approaching twilight. He therefore captured culture at its homeostatic stage: culture at the service of the status quo, of the monotonous reproduction of society and maintenance of system equilibrium, just before the inevitable and fast approaching loss of its position.

That loss of position was the result of a number of processes constituting the transformation of modernity from its 'solid' to its 'liquid' phase. I use the term 'liquid modernity' here for the currently existing shape of the modern condition, described by other authors as 'postmodernity', 'late modernity', 'second' or 'hyper' modernity. What makes modernity 'liquid', and thus justifies the choice of name, is its self-propelling, self-intensifying, compulsive and obsessive 'modernization', as a result of which, like liquid, none of the consecutive forms of social life is able to maintain its shape for long. 'Dissolving everything that is solid' has been the innate and defining characteristic of the modern form of life from the outset; but today, unlike yesterday, the dissolved forms are not to be replaced, and nor are they replaced, by other solid forms – deemed 'improved' in the sense of being even more solid and 'permanent' than those that came before them, and so even more resistant to melting. In the place of the melting, and so impermanent, forms come others, no less – if not more – susceptible to melting and therefore equally impermanent.

At least in that part of the planet where appeals for culture are formulated and broadcast, eagerly read and passionately debated, culture (dismissed earlier, let us remind ourselves, from the role of handmaiden to the self-determining and self-confirming nations, states and class hierarchies) quickly loses the function of a servant of the self-reproducing social hierarchy. The tasks culture had been entrusted with until then fell away one by one, were abandoned, or began to be fulfilled by other means, and with different tools. Released from the obligations imposed on it by its creators and operators, obligations consequent upon their initially missionary and later homeostatic role in society, culture is now able to focus on fulfilling individual needs, solving individual problems and struggles with the challenges and troubles of personal lives.

It can be said that in liquid modern times, culture (and most particularly, though not exclusively, its artistic sphere) is fashioned to fit individual freedom of choice and individual responsibility for that choice; and that its function is to ensure that the choice should be and will always remain a necessity and unavoidable duty of life, while the responsibility for the choice and its consequences remains where it has been placed by the liquid modern human condition – on the shoulders of the individual, now appointed to the position of chief manager of 'life politics' and its sole executive.

We are not speaking here of a paradigm shift or its modification; it is more accurate to speak of a beginning of a 'post-paradigm' era in the history of culture (and not only of culture). Although the term 'paradigm' has not yet disappeared from everyday vocabulary, it has joined the rapidly growing family of the 'zombie-categories' (as Ulrich Beck would put it), of categories which should be used *sous rature*, if, in the absence of suitable substitutes, we are unable to give them up just yet (as Jacques Derrida would prefer to say). Liquid modernity is an arena of constant battle till death, waged against every kind of paradigm – and in effect against all homeostatic devices serving conformism and routine, that is to say imposing monotony and maintaining predictability. This applies as much to the inherited paradigmatic concept of culture as to culture as such (that is to say, the sum total of man's artificial products, or the man-made 'nature surplus') which that concept attempted to capture, intellectually assimilate and render intelligible.

Culture today consists of offers, not prohibitions; propositions, not norms. As Bourdieu noted earlier, culture today is engaged in laying down temptations and setting up attractions, with luring and seducing, not with normative regulation; with PR rather than police supervision; with the production, sowing and planting of new needs and desires, rather than with duty. If there is anything in relation to which today's culture plays the role of a homeostat, it is not the conservation of the current state, but the overwhelming demand for constant change (although, as distinct from the phase of the enlightenment, change without direction, or in a direction not established in advance). One might say that it serves not so much the stratifications and divisions of society, as the turnover-oriented consumer market.

Ours is a consumers' society, in which culture, in common with the rest of the world experienced by consumers, manifests itself as a repository of goods intended for consumption, all competing for the unbearably fleeting and distracted attention of potential clients, all trying to hold that attention for more than just the blink of an eye. As we noted at the beginning, doing away with rigid standards and fastidiousness, the acceptance of all tastes with impartiality and without unequivocal preference, a 'flexibility' of preferences (today's politically correct name for spinelessness) as well as a temporariness and inconsequence of choice – is the mark of the strategy now recommended as the most sensible and right. The sign of belonging to a cultural elite today is maximum tolerance and minimal choosiness. Cultural snobbery consists of an ostentatious denial of snobbery. The principle of cultural elitism is omnivorousness – feeling at home in every cultural milieu, without considering any as a home, let alone the only home. A TV reviewer and critic in the British intellectual press praised a New Year's Eve programme, in 2007–8 for its promise 'to provide an array of musical entertainment to sate everyone's appetite'. 'The good thing', he explained, is that its universal appeal means you can dip in and out of the show depending on your preference.'[5] It is a praiseworthy and in itself admirable quality of cultural supply in a society in which networks replace structures, and an uninterrupted game of connecting to and disconnecting from those networks and the neverending sequence of connections and disconnections replace determination, allegiance and belonging.

The tendencies described here have yet another aspect: one of the consequences of liberating art from its past burden of fulfilling a weighty function is also the distance, often ironic or cynical, assumed from it by its creators as well as its recipients. Art, when it is spoken about, rarely inspires the sanctimonious or reverential tone so common in the past. There is no coming to blows. No raising of barricades. No flashing of knives. If there is any talk about the superiority of one art form over another, it is voiced without passion or verve; and condemnatory views and character assassinations are rarer than ever before. What hides behind this state of things is embarrassment, lack of self-confidence, a sense of disorientation: if artists have no great and momentous tasks to perform, if their creations serve no other purpose than to bring fortune and fame to a chosen few and entertainment and personal pleasure to their beneficiaries, then how are they to be judged except by the public hype that happens to accompany them at any given moment? As Marshall McLuhan deftly summarized this state of affairs, 'Art is anything that you can get away with.' Or as Damien Hirst, latter-day darling of the most fashionable London art galleries, and those who can afford to be their clients, admitted candidly on receiving the Turner Prize, Britain's prestigious art award: 'It's amazing what you can do with an E in A-level art, a twisted imagination and a chainsaw.'

The forces driving the gradual transformation of the concept of 'culture' into its liquid modern embodiment are the same forces which favour the freeing of markets from their non-economic limitations: mainly social, political and ethnic. A liquid modern, consumer-oriented economy relies on a surplus of its offerings, their rapid ageing and an untimely withering of their seductive powers. Since it is impossible to know in advance which of the offered goods or services will turn out to be sufficiently tempting to awaken the desire of consumers, the only way to sift reality from wishful thinking is by multiplying attempts and making costly mistakes. An uninterrupted supply of ever new offers is imperative for an increased turnover of goods, with a shortened time interval between their acquisition and their disposal, accompanied by their replacement with 'new and better' goods; it is imperative too for the avoidance of a situation in which yet another disappointment with specific goods risks turning into a general disappointment with a life woven embroidered with the yarn of consumer highs on a canvas of commercial networks.

Culture likens itself today to one of the departments of a world which has been fashioned into a gigantic department store experienced by people who have been turned into consumers first and foremost. As in the other departments of this megastore, its shelves are overflowing with attractions changed on a daily basis, and its counters are festooned with the latest promotions, which will vanish as instantly as the aging novelties they advertise. The goods displayed on the shelves, as well as the advertisements on the counters, are calculated to awaken irrepressible, but by nature momentary whims (as George Steiner famously put it, 'made for maximal impact and instant obsolescence'). The merchants of the goods and the authors of the advertisements depend on a marriage of the art of seduction with the impulse of potential clients to court the admiration of their peers and enjoy a sense of their own superiority.

To sum up, the culture of liquid modernity has no 'populace' to enlighten and ennoble; it does, however, have clients to seduce. Seduction, by contrast with enlightenment and ennoblement, is not a one-off, once and for all task, but an open-ended activity. The function of culture is not to satisfy existing needs, but to create new ones – while simultaneously maintaining needs already entrenched or permanently unfulfilled. Its chief concern is to prevent a feeling of satisfaction in its former subjects and charges, now turned into clients, and in particular to counteract their perfect, complete and definitive gratification, which would leave no room for further, new and as yet unfulfilled needs and whims.

2

On fashion, liquid identity and utopia for today – some cultural tendencies in the twenty-first century

'Fashion', according to Georg Simmel, 'never just is. It exists in a permanent state of becoming.' In sharp contrast to physical processes, and in common with the concept of *perpetuum mobile*, the eventuality of existing in a constant state of flux (that is, eternally performing its work) is not unthinkable in the case of fashion.

What is unthinkable, however, is the breaking of the chain of self-propagating change, once it is set in motion. Indeed, the most remarkable aspect of fashion is that its 'becoming' loses none of its momentum in the course of or as a result of 'doing its work' in the world in which it exists. The 'becoming' of fashion not only does not lose energy or momentum, but its driving force increases with its influence and with the accumulating evidence of its impact.

Were fashion to be merely a common physical process,

it would be a monstrous anomaly, breaking all the laws of nature. But fashion is not a physical fact: it is a social phenomenon.

Social life is by its very nature an extraordinary contrivance: it does all it can to invalidate the second law of thermodynamics by carving out for itself a niche safe from the curse of 'entropy', that is to say a 'thermodynamic quantity representing the sum of energy in the system that can't be used for mechanical work', this quantity 'growing with the degradation of matter and energy to their ultimate state of stagnant homogeneity'. In the case of fashion that state of inertia-inducing uniformity is not an 'ultimate state' but its opposite, an ever receding prospect: the more aspects of human endeavour and habitat are subjected to the logic of fashion, the more unattainable the regulation and stability of either. It is as if fashion were fitted with a safety valve which opens up long before the prospect of loss of energy resulting from conformity (the desire for which is, paradoxically, one of the basic human impulses keeping the process of fashion in its constant state of 'becoming') comes close enough to threaten fashion with slowing down, to say nothing of exhausting its power to tempt and seduce. If entropy is, so to speak, a leveller of diversity, so fashion (which, let us reiterate, draws its life force from the human disinclination for distinction and a desire for uniformity) multiplies and intensifies the very divisions, differences, inequalities, discriminations and handicaps which it promises to smooth away and ultimately eliminate altogether.

An impossibility in the physical universe, *perpetuum mobile* (a self-perpetuating process which gathers energy while expending it) becomes the norm the moment it finds itself in a 'socialized world'. How is this possible? Simmel asked the question, and he explains: it happens through the confrontation of two equally powerful and all-embracing human desires and yearnings – two inseparable yet constantly conflicting companions, their gazes trained in opposite directions. Borrowing again from the terminology of physics, we might say that the 'becoming' of fashion is something like a peculiar pendulum whose kinetic motion is gradually but thoroughly, without any loss, sometimes even with some gain, transformed into potential energy ready to change into the kinetic energy of contramotion. Pendulums oscillate, and if it weren't for the loss of energy with every change of direction, they would never stop.

The contradictory yearnings and desires spoken of here are a longing for a sense of belonging within a group or an agglomeration, and a desire to be distinct from the masses, to acquire a sense of individuality and originality; a dream of belonging and a dream of independence; the need for social support, and the demand for autonomy; a wish to be like everyone else, and a pursuit of uniqueness. In short, all these contradictions come down to the conflict between a need to hold hands because of a longing for safety, and a need to let go because of a longing for freedom. Or, if we look at this conflict from another perspective: the fear of being different, and the fear of losing individuality. Or of loneliness and of a lack of solitude.

As with (most?) marriages, safety and freedom cannot exist without one another, but coexistence does not come easily. Safety without freedom amounts to captivity, and freedom without safety instils chronic uncertainty and threatens a nervous breakdown. Should either be denied the redemptive effects of its balancing, compensating and neutralizing partner (or rather, alter ego), both safety and freedom turn from eagerly desired values into sleepless nightmares. Safety and freedom are mutually dependent, yet at the same time mutually exclusive. They attract and repel one another in unequal measure, the relative proportions of these contradictory feelings changing in step with the frequent (frequent enough to be deemed routine) deviations from the 'golden mean', for which the compromises attained (mostly not for long) between them are taken.

Any attempts to achieve balance and harmony between these desires or values usually turn out to be incomplete, not wholly satisfying, and also too unstable and fragile to bring an aura of certainty. There will always be some loose ends in need of tying up, though with each tug threatening to rip the gossamer-thin network of relationships. For this reason, attempts at conciliation never attain the aim so strenuously pursued, whether it is acknowledged or secret; for this reason, too, they are impossible to give up. The cohabitation of safety with freedom will always remain tempestuous and highly strung. Its intrinsic and unresolvable ambivalence is an inexhaustible source of creative energy and obsessive change. It is this which determines its status of *perpetuum mobile*.

'Fashion', says Simmel, 'is a particular form of life, which seeks to ensure a compromise between a tendency towards social equality and a tendency towards individual separateness'.[1] That compromise, we repeat, cannot be a 'permanent state', it cannot be fixed once and for all: the clause 'until further notice' is written into it with an indelible marker. This compromise, like fashion in search of it, never just 'is', it always 'becomes'. It cannot stand still; it requires continuous renegotiation. Driven by the impulse to be different and to escape the crowds and the rat race, the mass pursuit of the latest fashion (of the very moment), quickly causes the current marks of distinction to become common, vulgar and trivial, and even the shortest lapse of attention, or even a momentary slowing down of the speed of prestidigitation may produce effects opposite to those intended: the loss of individuality. Today's tokens of 'being ahead' have to be acquired quickly, while those of yesterday must be just as swiftly confined to the scrapheap. The injunction to keep an eye on 'what has already gone out of fashion' must be observed as conscientiously as the obligation to keep on top of what is (at this moment) new and up to date. The lifestyle declared by those enjoying or aspiring to it, communicated to others and made publicly recognizable by the acquisition of symbols of changing fashions, is defined equally by the prominence of symbols of the latest trends and by the absence of those no longer in fashion.

The *perpetuum mobile* of fashion is in effect a highly qualified, richly experienced and very efficient destroyer of all inertia. Fashion casts every lifestyle into a state of permanent, interminable revolution. Since the phenomenon of fashion is intimately and indissolubly bound up with the eternal and universal attributes of human ways in the world and their equally irremovable conflict, its appearance is not confined to one or a few chosen ways of life. In every period of history, in every territory of human habitation and in every culture, fashion has taken on the role of chief operator in the refashioning of constant change into a norm of the human way of life. Yet its modus operandi, in common with the institutions which serve its operations, changes with time. The current form of the phenomenon of fashion is defined by the colonization and exploitation by the consumer markets of that eternal aspect of human condition.

Fashion is one of the principal flywheels of 'progress' (that is to say, the kind of change which belittles and denigrates, in other words devalues, everything it leaves behind and replaces with something new). But in sharp opposition to earlier uses of this term, the word 'progress', as it appears on commercial internet sites, is associated less with a hope of escape from peril than with a threat from which to seek escape; it does not define the objective of exertion but the reason for its necessity. In today's use of the term, 'progress' is primarily an unstoppable process which takes place with no regard for our wishes and with indifference to our feelings – a process whose unstoppable and overpowering force demands our meek submission according to the principle of 'if you can't beat them, join them'. Progress, according to the beliefs instilled by the consumer markets, is a mortal threat to the lazy, the imprudent and the slothful. The imperative of 'joining progress' or 'following progress' is inspired by a wish to escape from the spectre of personal catastrophe caused by impersonal, social factors whose breath can be constantly felt on one's neck. What it evokes is the case of the 'flight into the future' of the Angel of History in the painting by Paul Klee commented on by Walter Benjamin: an angel with his back to the future, into which he is pushed by the revulsion he feels at the sight of the decaying and malodorous remains left behind from previous escapes

. . . only here, to paraphrase Marx, the epic tragedy of the Angel of History is shaped by market-driven fashion into the mould of a cameral grotesque.

Progress, in short, has moved from a discourse of the shared improvement of life to a discourse of personal survival. Progress is no longer thought of in the context of a desire for speed, but in the context of a desperate effort not to fall off the track and to avoid disqualification and exclusion from the race. We think of 'progress' in the context not of raising our status, but of avoiding failure. You hear the news, for instance, that Brazil will be 'the only sunny winter destination' this year, and you conclude that this year you cannot be seen in places where people who share your aspirations were seen last year. Or you read that you must 'get rid of a poncho' which was very in vogue last year, because when you wear it today it makes you look (since time does not stand still) 'like a camel'. What is more, you learn that pinstriped suits and t-shirts which were 'a must' last season are so yesterday today, because today 'everybody and anybody is wearing them' . . . and so on. Time is indeed passing, and the trick is to keep pace with it. If you don't want to drown, you must keep on surfing: that is to say, keep changing, as often as you can, your wardrobe, furniture, wallpaper, appearance and habits, in short – yourself.

Once the concerted and resourceful efforts of the consumer market have enabled culture to be subjugated to the logic of fashion, it becomes necessary – in order to be oneself and be seen as such – to prove one's ability to be someone else. The personal model in one's search for identity becomes that of the chameleon. Or of the legendary Prometheus, whose mythical ability to transform at will into any other entity, or to take on random forms, however distinct from the original, were so admired in the Renaissance by Pico della Mirandola. Today's all-encompassing culture demands that you acquire the ability to change your identity (or at least its public manifestation) as often, as fast and as efficiently as you change your shirt or your socks. And for a modest, or not so modest, price, the consumer market will assist you in the acquisition of this skill in obedience to culture's recommendation.

I need not add, since it should be obvious, that the shift of focus from possessing to throwing away, scrapping and disposing of things fits perfectly with the logic of a consumer-oriented economy. People who hold on to yesterday's clothes, computers and mobile phones could spell catastrophe for an economy whose main concern, and the *sine qua non* of survival, is the fast, and ever faster, disposal of purchased and acquired goods onto the rubbish heap; an economy whose vertebral column is rubbish disposal.

Escape ranks as the most popular (and in reality a mandatory) pursuit. Armies no longer insist on compulsory military service – they even shun it; yet the common duty of a citizen/consumer, a duty sanctioned by capital (social) punishment for desertion, is to remain faithful to fashion and to continue being fashionable. Semantically speaking, escape is the opposite of utopia, yet psychologically it turns out to be the only substitute for it available today: one might say, that it is utopia's new, up-to-date interpretation, adapted to the demands of our deregulated, individualized society of consumers. It is obvious today that you can no longer seriously entertain any real hope of making the world a nicer place to live in; but you might just be tempted to safeguard (from fashion, from 'progress'), at least for a while, that relatively pleasant, private place which you have managed to carve out for yourself in that world.

Our private concerns and efforts mainly boil down to the avoidance of failure. The fight for survival demands our complete, undivided attention, around-the-clock vigil, seven days a week – and above all constant movement, as fast as is possible . . .

Sławomir Mrożek, the renowned Polish writer familiar with many cultures, has observed: 'Once upon a time, we blamed our unhappiness on the management of the day – God. We concurred that he ran the business badly. We sacked him and appointed ourselves managers'.[2] But, noted Mrożek, a staunch anticlerical, business did not improve with the managerial changes. It did not improve because when our dreams and hopes for a better life are concentrated entirely on our own egos, and are reduced to a tinkering with our bodies or souls, 'there are no limits to our ambitions and temptations, and so for the ego to grow, all limitations must go'. . . 'I was told: "Make it up yourself, devise your own life, arrange it just how you like it, not only minute by minute but from start to finish." But can I do this? Just like that, without help, rehearsals, trials, mistakes and corrections, above all, without doubts?'[3] The pain of punitively limited choice was replaced by another pain, no less severe, this time however occasioned by the duty of making an irrevocable choice in the face of uncertainty – and lack of confidence in the efficacy of any subsequent choices. Mrożek sees a close similarity between the world we live in and a fancy-dress stall, 'surrounded by a throng of people searching for their own "self" . . . you can change endlessly, what unlimited freedom . . . so let's search for our "self", what fun – on condition that we never find it. Then the party would be over.'[4]

The singular idea of divesting uncertainty of its power to disable, and making happiness into a permanent and safe condition (by a continuous and unbroken varying of one's 'self' by means of changing costumes), is the very embodiment of utopia today. It is not only a utopia inherently suited to a society of 'hunters' (who have replaced the 'gardeners', protagonists of the era of 'solid' modernity, and the 'gamekeepers' of premodern times), it is also a utopia which caters to such a society; a 'deregulated', 'privatized', 'individualized' version of the old dream of a 'good society', that is to say, an environment hospitable to the humanity of its members and one which guarantees that humanity.

Hunting is a full-time occupation on the stage of liquid modernity. It consumes an inordinate amount of attention and energy, leaving little time for anything else. It distracts attention from the inherent endlessness of the task and defers *ad calendas graecas* – to a non-existing date – the moment of reflection and the face-to-face realization of the impossibility of its completion. As Blaise Pascal noted several centuries ago, people search only for urgent and overwhelming occupations which can stop them from thinking solely about themselves, and for that reason they make their goal some attractive object which can charm and seduce them. People wish to escape the need to think of their 'unhappy condition': 'this is why we prefer the hunt to the capture'; 'the have itself would not save us from thinking of death and the miseries distracting us, but hunting does so.'⁵ Pascal's thoughts are made real today through the agency of commercialized fashion.

Hunting is like a drug: once tasted, it turns into a habit, an inner necessity and an obsession. The hunting down of a rabbit is sure to be an unpleasant disappointment, and it will make the temptation of a further chase even more difficult to resist, because the expectation of a successful hunt will turn out to be the most delicious (the only delicious?) experience of the whole event. The hunting down of a rabbit puts an end to the excitement – enhancing expectations; the only method of assuaging frustration is immediately to plan and commence the next hunting escapade.

Is this the end of utopia? In one sense it is: early modern utopian thought was inspired by the desire for a rest from the disabling and fear-inducing chaos of events – a dream of reaching the end of an obstacle race, of unbearable hardships, and a dream of the nirvana lying on the other side of the finishing line, where time stands still and history is denied access. There is no room in the life of a hunter, however, for a moment when it can be said with certainty that the task is finished, the case closed, mission accomplished – a moment, in other words, when the only expectation is rest and unmitigated pleasure in the accumulated spoils.

In a society of hunters, the prospect of the end of the chase is not beguiling, it is horrifying: it would, after all, be a moment of personal failure. Hunting horns would be calling again to new adventures, hounds would be howling, reawakening delicious dreams of hunts gone by; all around, others would be in hot pursuit of their prey, there would be no end of excitement and joyful clamour . . . I alone would be sidelined, excluded and driven out from the company, unwanted and denied the fun; a person allowed to watch the frolics of others from behind a fence, but denied the chance to take part. If the life of the hunt is the utopia for our times, it is, in contrast to its precursors, a utopia of adventure without end. It is indeed a strange utopia. Its antecedents were lured by the prospect of the end of the road and of toil, while the utopia of hunters is a dream in which the road and the toil never end. It is not the journey's end that stokes the effort, it is its infinitude.

It is a strange and unorthodox utopia, but utopia it is, like the others before it, promising what is, after all, an unattainable reward, a definitive and radical solution to all human problems, past, present and future, and a definitive and radical antidote to all the ills and woes of the human condition. It is an unorthodox utopia in that it brings forth a land of solutions and cures from the 'there and then' of the distant future to the 'here and now' of the present moment. Instead of a life towards utopia, hunters are offered a life in utopia. For 'gardeners' utopia was the end of the road, while for 'hunters' the road itself is the utopia. (Should we not, in this case, exchange the term 'u-topia' for the term 'u-via'?)

Gardeners saw in the end of the road the realization and the final triumph of utopia. For the hunters, reaching the end of the road would constitute utopia's final and ignominious defeat. Humiliation would be added to the existing grievances, thus turning this setback into a personal defeat. Since other hunters will not cease hunting, exclusion from the continuing hunt will become tantamount to disgrace and the shame of rejection: and in the final analysis, to the ignominy of the exposure of one's own inadequacy.

Utopia brought forth from a nebulous elsewhere to the tangible 'here and now', utopia already lived rather than 'aspired to', is immune to the test of future experiences. It is to all intents and purposes immortal. But it earned its immortality at the expense of the fragility and susceptibility of everyone it had ever charmed and seduced. This, approximately speaking, is the basis of the phenomenon of fashion. We might as well have been speaking of fashion here, rather than of liquid modern life and its utopia . . .

In contrast to utopias of old, the utopia of liquid modernity, the utopia, or 'u-via', of hunters, the utopia of life revolving around the pursuit of constantly elusive fashion, does not give sense to life, whether authentic or fake. It merely helps to banish the question of life's meaning from our minds. Having turned life's journey into a neverending series of egotistical measures, making each episode experienced into an introduction to the next in the series, it does not offer an opportunity to consider its direction, or life's meaning as such. When such an opportunity finally presents itself, that is at moments of dropping out of, or being excluded from the hunter's way of life, it is as a rule too late for reflection to influence the course of one's life and the life of those around. It is too late to object to the 'actually existing' shape of one's life, and certainly for any questioning of its sense to bring practical results.

The study of fashion, identity problems or the metamorphosis of utopia are just some of the 'grains of sand' in which William Blake attempted to 'see the world'; that is, a way to 'hold infinity in the palm of your hand', and hold it tight. The world to be glimpsed in these few grains of sand is the world we all inhabit together, natives of the liquid modern epoch. And that infinity captured in the course of our reflections is our *Lebenswelt*, the world of our experiences, that is, a world experienced by us; a world shaped by our and other artists' way of life within it, under culture's historical decree.

3

Culture from nation-building to globalization

The contours of the cultural scene which were to 'dissolve in the darkness of twilight' as Pierre Bourdieu's owl took flight (as mentioned in the chapter above) were those noted and described through the prism of the 'self-balancing system' aspired to, hailed and prematurely and periodically celebrated and feted by the scholars and expert panegyrists of the nation-states of the 'solid' phase of the modern era. Since well functioning homeostatic devices (devices which make any deflection from the chosen system model difficult, or even impossible, and which restore its interrupted routines) are essential for the survival of long-lasting and immutable systems, the impulse to define and judge all elements or aspects of society in terms of their homeostatic qualities and effects was the natural tendency of those societies identifying with or aspiring to these systems.

While nation-states fostered such aspirations and hopes, to favour homeostatic qualities seemed as well founded as it was inevitable, and it seemed irrefutably obvious to accept its stabilizing effects on a system as the criterion of the 'functionality' (read, the usefulness and desirability) of the phenomenon causing them. From the moment that nation-states began to be coerced, encouraged and inclined to abandon those aspirations and hopes, however, the fundamentals of these practices became not quite so unshakeable: the measurement of the 'functionality' (I repeat, the usefulness and desirability) of institutions based on their stabilizing effect on the system no longer appeared so indisputable or undeniably correct.

For as long as aspirations for a system's monotonous self-recreation lived on (but no longer), the homeostatic vision of culture remained immune to criticism. But aspirations began to weaken, and eventually, under the pressure of globalization, had to be abandoned altogether – reluctantly at first, but soon without major doubts, and indeed willingly. A side-effect of the loss of aspirations was the gradual emergence of the flimsy, indistinct, fragile and ultimately fictitious nature of system boundaries; and in the end the passing away of illusion of territorial sovereignty, and with it the tendency to endorse a nation-state according to the strength of its self-sufficient, self-reproducing and self-balancing system.

The profound consequences of the influence of globalization (above all, the mutual separation of power and politics, and the subsequent relinquishment by the weakened state of its traditional functions, freeing them from political supervision) have been thoroughly examined and minutely described in sociological and political literature. Let us therefore limit ourselves here to just one aspect of the globalization process, one all too rarely discussed in the context of the changing paradigm of research and cultural theory: that is to say, the altering character of global migration.

Mass migration, or the migration of people (as opposed to peoples, as was the case in the early Middle Ages), was an integral part of modernity and modernization, of its way of life, continuously and from the very beginning – and no wonder, considering that order creation and economic growth, two worthy components of modernization, gave rise to growing groups of people branded as superfluous in their homelands: the waste from order creation and the waste from economic growth. Three separate phases make up the history of modern migration.

The first was the emigration of about 60 million people from Europe, the only 'modernizing area of the planet at the time (that is to say, the only 'overpopulated' terrain), to 'empty lands' (meaning those lands whose indigenous populations the overpopulated and mighty Europe could overlook, or regard as non-existent or irrelevant to its future plans and calculations). Whatever might remain of the native populations after the onslaught of mass killings, and equally mass epidemics, would become for the newcomers yet another case for 'cultivation', to be dealt with in the manner already tried at home by their own cultural elite – now raised to the rank of the 'white man's mission'.

The second wave turned the direction of the original imperial migration by 180 degrees. With the decline of colonial empires, some of the native populations – with varying degrees of education and 'cultural sophistication' – followed the colonialists returning to their homelands; they settled in cities where they were to be fitted into the only worldview and strategic model available to date, the model of assimilation, created in the early phase of nation-building as a way of dealing with ethnic minorities, linguistic or cultural. For the sake of their assimilation, intended to unify the nation being shaped under the aegis of a modern state, the newcomers were turned into 'minorities' (though admittedly with ever diminishing conviction, eagerness or chances of success), into the subjects of cultural crusades, *Kulturkampf* and proselytizing missions. This second phase in the history of modern migration has not yet come to an end. More out of inertia than any discernment of the new situation, its echoes still resound every now and then in public declarations of intent by politicians (though in the spirit of political correctness, they are more often than not passed off as demands for 'civic education' or 'integration').

The third phase of modern migration, currently in full flow and gathering momentum despite frenetic attempts to hold it back, introduces the age of diasporas: an infinite archipelago of ethnic, religious and linguistic settlements, heedless of the pathways marked out and paved by the imperial/colonial episode, and steered instead by the logic of the global redistribution of living resources and the chances of survival peculiar to the current stadium of globalization. Diasporas are dispersed and scattered over many formally sovereign territories; they ignore native pretensions to the primacy of local needs, demands and entitlements, and toss about in the snares of dual (or multi) citizenship – and, what is more dual (or multiple) loyalty. The migration of today differs from its earlier phases in the equity of its many possible pathways – and in the fact that almost no country today is exclusively a place of immigration or emigration. No longer unequivocally predetermined by the heritage of the imperial/colonial past, the pathways of migration are formed and re-formed ad hoc.

The latest phase of migration poses a question mark over the incipient and unbreakable bond between identity and nationality, the individual and her or his place of habitation, physical neighbourhood and cultural identity (or more simply, physical and cultural proximity). Jonathan Rutherford, the perceptive and clear-sighted observer of the flexible boundaries of human community, notes that the residents of the London street where he lives belong to a neighbourhood of communities widely different from one another in terms of their culture, language and customs: from small agglomerations crowded together inside the limits of just a few neighbouring streets, to the outposts of far-flung, sometimes truly vast networks. It is a neighbourhood of meandering, spongy and porous boundaries, in which it is difficult to ascertain who legally belongs and who is a stranger, who is at home, and who is an intruder. Where do we belong when we live in a neighbourhood like this one, asks Rutherford, leaving the question unanswered. What is this thing we call home? And when we look back and remember what brought us here, which of the tales told and heard by us do we feel most connected to?[1]

The lives of many, perhaps the majority of us Europeans are lived today in diaspora (how far-reaching and in what direction(s)?) or among diasporas (how far-reaching and in what direction(s)?). For the first time the 'art of living with difference' has become an everyday problem. This problem could materialize only at a point when the differences between people had ceased to be perceived merely as transitory irritants. Unlike in the past, the reality of living in close proximity with strangers seems to be here to stay, and so it demands that skills in daily coexistence with ways of life other than our own must be worked out or acquired; a coexistence, what is more, which will prove not only bearable but mutually beneficial – not just despite, but because of the differences dividing us. The notion of 'human rights' promoted today as a replacement for the idea of territorially determined rights (and, in practice, territorially limited rights) or, so to speak, the 'rights of belonging', is after all, in the last analysis, the right to difference.

The new interpretation of the notion of basic human rights lays the foundations, at the very least, for mutual tolerance; it categorically does not, however, go so far as to lay the foundations for mutual solidarity. The new interpretation breaks down the hierarchy of cultures inherited from the past, and tears apart the model of assimilation as a naturally 'progressive' cultural evolution heading inexorably towards a predetermined model goal. Axiologically speaking, cultural relations are no longer vertical but horizontal: no culture can demand or be entitled to subservience, humility or submission on the part of any other simply on account of its own assumed superiority or 'progressiveness'. Ways of life today drift in varied and not necessarily coordinated directions; they come into contact and separate, they approach and distance themselves from one another, embrace and repel, enter into conflict, or initiate a mutual exchange of experience or services – and they do all this (to paraphrase Simmel's memorable phrase) floating in a suspension of cultures, all of a similar, or of a wholly identical specific gravity. Supposedly stable and unquestionable hierarchies and one-directional evolutionary pathways are today replaced by contentions for the permission to be different: these are clashes and battles whose outcomes are impossible to predict and whose conclusiveness cannot be relied on.

Following the example of Archimedes, who purportedly promised to turn the world upside down if only a suitable point of support could be found, we can say that we might have been able to predict correctly who would assimilate whom, whose singularity and uniqueness was destined to disappear and whose to come into its own, or even dominate, if only we had been presented with an unequivocal and uncontested hierarchy of cultures. Well, we are not being presented with one, and nor it would seem are we likely to be presented with one in any foreseeable future.

The scale of today's global population movements is vast and keeps on growing. Governments strain their inventiveness to the limit to find favour with the electorate by limiting immigrants' access or their rights to asylum, or more generally rights to shelter and hardship assistance – yet despite their efforts, the chances of the current version of the 'great migration of peoples' coming to an early end remain slim. Politicians and the lawyers they hire do what they can to draw a line between the free passage of capital, currency and investment, and the welcomed people of business who follow in their wake, and the job-seeking migrants towards whom they have an undisguised animosity, successfully competing in this respect with their electorate; such a line is not easy to draw, however, and it is even harder to fortify and make impenetrable. The eagerness of consumers and the enthusiasm of investors would soon wane if the freedom of commercial turnover were not matched by a freedom of the workforce (and so also the potential demand for goods) to follow where both – work and consumerist possibilities – await them.

It is impossible to deny that freely moving 'market forces' contribute enormously to the increased mobility of 'economic' migrants. Yet even territorial governments are occasionally, if reluctantly, obliged to cooperate with them. Both forces are jointly favourable to processes which at least one of them would in practice, even more than in theory, prefer to arrest in the hope of political gain. According to research conducted by Saskia Sassen, the actions of exterritorial agencies, as well as those of local governments, regardless of what their spokespeople may say, on the whole intensify migration rather than reduce it.[2] After the destruction of traditional local trade, people deprived of income or any hope of regaining it become easy prey for quasi-official criminal organizations specializing in 'live trade'. In the 1990s criminal organizations earned about $3.5 billion per annum from illegal migration – and tacit support from governments 'looking the other way' was not unheard of. When the Philippines, for instance, tried to balance the state budget and pay off part of government debt from the profitable export of human surplus, the governments of the United States and Japan passed laws permitting the import of foreign workers (that is to say, people on the whole less demanding than locals) into jobs suffering from a serious dearth of local workers prepared to agree to the proposed scales of pay and to offer their labour for a pittance.

The joint outcome of all these pressures is the global growth of ethnic diasporas; people are on the whole much less volatile than the economic cycles of growth and crisis, and every consecutive cycle leaves behind it settlements of immigrants who endeavour to domesticate themselves in the country to which they have been brought. Even if the recent arrivals wanted to follow the boom and move on, the self-same complications of migration law which brought them to the country without so much as a hitch would now prove impossible to overcome. Immigrants have no choice in practice but to accept the fate of being yet another 'ethnic minority' in the country to which they have come; for natives, there is nothing left but to prepare themselves for a lifetime spent surrounded by diasporas. Both are expected to find ways to cope with unfavourable realities over which they have no control.

At the end of his in-depth study of one such diaspora in Great Britain, Geoff Dench suggests:

> Many people in Britain . . . do regard ethnic minorities as outsiders whose destinies and loyalties are self-evidently different from those of the British people, and whose dependent and inferior standing in Britain goes without saying. Wherever a conflict of interests arises it is axiomatic that public sympathy should be against them . . .[3]

These generalizations apply not only to Great Britain, and not only to the single 'ethnic minority' (the Maltese) which was the main object of Dench's study. Similar tendencies are noted in every country where such diasporas have appeared, in other words the length and breadth of the planet. The close proximity of 'ethnically foreign' agglomerations releases tribal moods in the local population, and the purpose of strategies insinuated by these moods is a ghetto-minded, compulsory isolation of 'foreign elements', which in turn magnifies the defensive impulses of the incoming populations: their inclination towards estrangement and self-enclosure in circles of their own. Such a mutual feeding of pressures and impulses has all the characteristics of a 'schismatic chain' as described by Gregory Bateson, known for its tendency to self-propel and self-intensify – and always difficult to stop, let alone sever. Tendencies towards separation and fencing off appear on both sides, adding arguments and passion.

However lamented by numerous liberally minded and influential bodies this state of affairs may be, no policy-makers seem to come forward who are genuinely interested in putting a stop to the Catch 22 situation of mutually inciting isolationist pressures, let alone in seriously undertaking to eliminate their sources. On the other hand, many other mighty powers conspire to erect barricades from both sides, and more still collaborate stealthily, and sometimes unwittingly and involuntarily, in their construction and in the deployment of armed troops.

There is first of all an old tried and tested adage of 'divide and rule' which authorities of all epochs have willingly reached for as soon as they have felt threatened by an accumulation and concentration of varied and dispersed grievances, resentments and grudges. If only it were possible to prevent all the doubts and protests of the wronged from flowing together into a single stream; to ensure that each category of the downtrodden would grapple with their own particular and singular type of oppression separately and single-handedly, suspiciously eyeing other unfortunates doing the same. It might then be possible to direct the flow of emotions towards different outlets, and to break up, disperse and exhaust the energy of the protest in a mass of intertribal and intercommunal scuffles. Guardians of the law might be able to don the vestments of impartial moderators and come forward in the role of advocates of the conciliation of group interests, evangelists of peaceful coexistence and devotees of an end to animosities and mutually destructive wars; while at the same time their original role in causing the state of affairs which made the commencement of hostilities unavoidable would be removed from sight and passed over in silence. Richard Rorty offers a 'thick description' (Clifford Geertz's expression) of the contemporary uses for this time-honoured strategy:

> The aim will be to keep the minds of the proles elsewhere – to keep the bottom 75 percent of Americans and the bottom 95 percent of the world's population busy with ethnic and religious hostilities, and with debates about sexual mores. If the proles can be distracted from their own despair by media-created pseudo-events, including the occasional brief and bloody wars, the super rich will have little to fear.[4]

When the poor lock horns with the poor, the rich have every reason to rub their hands with glee. It is not just that the danger of them turning on those responsible for their suffering will be averted indefinitely, as it has been in the past whenever the principle of 'divide and rule' has been cleverly and effectively implemented; today there are new reasons to rejoice, specific to our times, conditioned as they are by the new character of the global power setting. Global powers today use a strategy of distance and non-engagement, made possible by the speed with which they are able to move, slipping effortlessly and without warning out of the grasp of local authorities, easily escaping even the densest of nets, leaving to the warring native tribes the ungrateful task of toiling for a truce, healing wounds and clearing the rubble.

The ease of movement of the elite in the planetary 'space of flows' (as the world in which the life of the global elite is inscribed was defined by Manuel Castells) depends to a great extent on the inability or unwillingness of the 'natives' (or people fixed by contrast in a 'space of localities') to act with solidarity. The more discordant their relationships and the more dispersed the natives, the more numerous and slimmer their warring factions, the more passion they invest in fighting their equally weak opponents from the neighbourhood, the smaller is the chance that they will ever bring themselves to unite and close ranks. It is even less likely that they would ever join forces to avert retaliation: yet another escape of capital, liquidation of places of employment and annihilation of their livelihood.

Contrary to frequently held opinion, the absence of political bodies capable of matching the might of world economic powers is not just a question of their relatively late development; this is not about the fact that existing political institutions have not as yet had time to unite or to subscribe to a new global, democratically supervised system of restraints and counterweights. On the contrary, it seems that the breaking up of the public ground, charging it with intercommunal conflict, is the very political infrastructure demanded by the new global power hierarchy for the practice of the strategy of non-engagement – and that the global powers placed at the peak of this hierarchy, reaching the 'space of flows', will openly, or secretly, but always assiduously and attentively, cultivate, as long as they are allowed to, a disunity of dramaturgy and a desynchronization of the lines assigned to the cast. In order for there to be nothing to worry about, the managers of the global order need an inexhaustible abundance of local unrest.

In my quote from Rorty, I omitted to mention his allusion to 'debate about sexual mores' as another factor – alongside 'ethnic and religious hostilities' – responsible for the fact that the 'super-rich' 'have little to fear'. This was an allusion to the 'cultural left', which, for all its merits in combating a sadism-tinged animosity towards the breaking of cultural moulds so common in American society, is in Rorty's opinion guilty of deleting from the list of public concerns that of material poverty, the deepest source of all manner of inequalities and injustices. The sin of the 'cultural left', Rorty claims, is its placing of material handicap on a par with mutual pointing out of one another's deviations by different factions of disadvantaged minorities, and their inclination to see lifestyle differences as a case in point. Rorty rebukes the American 'cultural left' for treating all aspects of inequality as though they were a question of cultural difference, and thus in the last analysis as symptoms and consequences of the differences in human choices, protected after all by human rights and by the ethical demand for tolerance; for its acceptance of all difference as equally praiseworthy and worth safeguarding simply by virtue of being different from others; and so also for the fact that all discussion of the merits of difference, however serious, honest and mutually respectful, must, according to cultural left, be

avoided, even forbidden, if the aim is to reconcile existing differences sufficiently for everyday living standards
to be raised onto a higher (and by implication better)
level.

Jonathan Friedman has called the intellectuals
professing views similar to those criticized by Rorty
'modernists without modernism': that is to say, in keeping with venerable modern tradition, sworn enthusiasts
of the transgression of status quo and the remodelling
of current realities, yet, not in keeping with the principles of modernism, devoid of a goal towards which
such transgressions or remodelling could (or should)
lead, and eliminating in advance any consideration of
its nature. In its practical consequences, the philosophy
of 'multiculturalism', so fashionable among 'modernists
without modernism', refutes its own theoretically prom-
ulgated value, of a harmonious (convivial?) coexistence
of cultures. Consciously or involuntarily, purposefully
or through neglect, this philosophy supports separatist
and therefore antagonistic tendencies, thereby making
even more difficult any attempt at serious multicultural
dialogue – the only activity that could slow down, or
overcome altogether, the currently chronic fragility of
the powers called on to effect social change.

The popularity of the attitudes criticized by Rorty
or Friedman is not surprising. The spreading of such
viewpoints was only to be expected, given the tendency
of the contemporary intellectual elite to reject their role
as educators, leaders and teachers – assigned to them
and expected by them in the era of nation-building –
in favour of another role, one emulating the business
faction of the global elite in its strategy of secession,
outdistancing and non-engagement. The vast majority

of intellectuals today want and look for 'more space' for themselves. Engagement in the affairs of 'another', as opposed to an indifferent resignation to their existence, would shrink that space instead of enlarging it. It would mean a commitment to bothersome and labour-intensive obligations, a limitation of freedom of movement, and the exposure of one's own interests to the vagaries of fate – it would therefore be an imprudent and thoroughly undesirable step for everyone involved.

The new indifference to difference presents itself in theory as an approval of 'cultural pluralism': the political practice formed and supported by this theory is defined by the term 'multiculturalism'. It is apparently inspired by the postulate of liberal tolerance and of support for communities' rights to independence and to public acceptance of their chosen (or inherited) identities. In reality, however, it acts as a socially conservative force. Its achievement is the transformation of social inequality, a phenomenon highly unlikely to win general approval, into the guise of 'cultural diversity', that is to say, a phenomenon deserving of universal respect and careful cultivation. Through this linguistic measure, the moral ugliness of poverty magically turns, as if by the touch of a fairy's wand, into the aesthetic appeal of cultural diversity. The fact that any struggle for recognition is doomed to failure so long as it is not supported by the practice of redistribution gets lost from view along the way. As does the fact that calls for respect of cultural differences bring little comfort to the many communities that are deprived of the power of independence by virtue of their handicap, and doomed to have their 'own' choices made by other, more substantial powers.

Alain Touraine proposed that the notion of 'multi-culturalism', born of respect for untrammelled freedom of choice from among the riches of cultural offerings, should be distinguished from something fundamentally (if not directly, then at least in its consequence) different: a programme which is best termed 'multicom-munitarianism'.[5] If the first notion assumes respect for the right of an individual to choose his or her mode of life and points of reference for his or her loyalty, so the other notion by contrast assumes that the loyalty of the individual is a question answered in advance by the irrefutable fact of belonging to a community of origin – a fact which makes the negotiation of life values and lifestyle useless. The mixing up of these two trends in the multiculturalism credo is as misleading and as potentially detrimental for human coexistence and collaboration as it is common.

For as long as the confusion between the two notions continues, the idea of 'multiculturalism' plays into the hand of a 'negative' – wild, unsupervised – globalization. Thanks to it, global forces can get away with the destructive consequences of their actions rising intra- and intersocial inequalities. The once common custom, openly arrogant and disdainful of the underprivileged, of explaining social deprivations by the inborn inferiority of the disadvantaged race has been replaced by a 'politically correct' interpretation of glaringly uneven living conditions as being the result of a multiplicity of lifestyle choices, the incontestable right of every community. The new culturalism, like racism before it, strives to stifle moral conscience and to accept human inequality by regarding it as a fact exceeding the capabilities of human intervention (in the case of racism) or as a condition which should not be interfered with, in deference to its venerable cultural values.

Let us add here that a certain similarity existed between the racist interpretation of inequality and the typical modern project of a 'perfect social order': the creation of order is by its very nature a selective activity, and so one had to accept that the 'lower races', those unable to meet adequate human standards, would not find a place in any nearly perfect order. The appearance and popularity of the new 'cultural' interpretation ties in, on the other hand, with a relinquishing of the modern quest for a 'perfect society'. In the absence of any prospects for a fundamental revision of the social order, it is clear that every human group is obliged single-handedly to find its own place in reality's liquid structures, and to bear the consequences of its choice. The 'cultural' interpretation, like its predecessor, passes over in silence the fact that social inequality is a vastly self-fulfilling phenomenon and that the representation of multiplying social divisions born of inequality as the inevitable product of free choice, rather than as a troublesome barrier to free choice, is one of the principal factors in its consolidation.

'Multiculturalism' is the answer most frequently given today by the educated, influential and politically significant classes when they are asked which values to cultivate and what direction to follow in our uncertain times. This answer is raised to the rank of a canon of 'political correctness', and furthermore it turns into an axiom which requires neither foundation nor proof; a peculiar prologomena to all further considerations of choices of political line, a cornerstone doxa, that is to say, knowledge with the help of which we think, but which rarely, if ever, itself becomes the subject of our thoughts.

In the case of the educated classes, today's variant, or mutant, of modern intellectuals, seeing multiculturalism as a solution to the problems afflicting the world of diasporas signals an attitude which can be summarized as follows: 'We are sorry, but we cannot get you out of the quagmire which you got yourself into.' It is true that chaos reigns in the world of values, as it does in debates on the meaning or correct forms of human coexistence, but you must unravel or cut this Gordian knot yourself using your own wits and bearing your own responsibility, and you will have only yourself to blame if the result is not to your liking. It is true that with the existing cacophony, no melody can possibly be sung in unison, and if you do not know either which melody is more worth singing than all the others, or how to find this out, then you are left with no other option than to sing your own choice of melody, or even, if you can, compose it yourself. The cacophony is already deafening enough for this not to make it any worse; one more melody will change nothing.

Russell Jacoby gave the title of *The End of Utopia* to his trenchant analysis of the emptiness of 'multicultural' confession of faith.[6] This title contains a message: the contemporary educated classes have little or nothing to say about the desirable shape of the human condition. For that reason they seek refuge in multiculturalism, that 'ideology of the end of ideology'.

Standing up to the status quo demands courage, considering the terrifying might of the powers supporting it; courage, however, is a quality which intellectuals, once known for their bravura, or downright heroic fearlessness, have lost in their dash for new roles and 'niches' as experts, academic gurus and media celebrities. It is tempting to see this modern version of *la trahison des clercs* as a sufficient explanation for the puzzle of the sudden resignation of educated classes from joint responsibility for and active involvement in human affairs.

We must resist this temptation, however. Hidden behind the indifference to all matters beyond those of business or caste interests are reasons which are more important than the actual or assumed cowardice of the educated elite, or its growing preference for personal convenience. The educated classes were never, and still aren't, alone in such wrongdoing. They journeyed towards their current standpoint in substantial company: alongside the growing exterritorial economic powers, in the midst of societies which ever more strongly and ever more unilaterally engage their members in the role of consumers of goods (consumers caring more about the size of their own slice of bread than the size of the whole loaf) rather than in the role of producers responsible for the quantity or quality of those goods – and in a rapidly individualized world, leaving individuals to find their own way of coping with socially created troubles. It was on that journey that the descendants of modern intellectuals underwent a transformation not unlike that which befell the rest of their fellow travellers.

4
Culture in a world of diasporas

The modern 'educated classes' (intellectuals *avant la lettre*, since the concept of 'intellectuals', a category united by a shared vocation to articulate, teach and defend national values, was not formed until the dawn of the twentieth century) constituted from the first a category of people with a mission. That mission was formulated in different ways, but in the most general terms the vocation assigned to them in the epoch of the Enlightenment and upheld by them ever since has been an active, perhaps merely helpful, yet decisive role in 're-rooting' what was 'uprooted' (or, in the terminology currently favoured by sociologists, in a renewed 'inclusion' of what was 'excluded'). This mission consisted of two tasks.

The first task, formulated by the philosophers of the Enlightenment at a time of the unstoppable disintegration and atrophy of the ancien régime (the 'old order' later renamed 'premodern') consisted of 'enlightening' or 'cultivating' 'the people'. The aim was to transform the disorientated, dismayed and lost entities – brutally torn out of their monotonous routine of communal life by the elemental and unexpected, rather than planned or anticipated modernizing transformation – into members of a modern nation and citizens of a modern state. The aim of enlightenment and culture was no less than the creation of a 'new man', equipped with new points of reference and flexible, adaptable standards in place of the lifelong rules hitherto imposed by traditional communities, from cradle to grave, which in the dawn of the modern era were gradually but implacably losing their pragmatic value, or falling out of use at an accelerated rate. According to the pioneers of Enlightenment, these rules for life, entrenched in tradition, were becoming a hindrance rather than a help in the new conditions. It did not matter that under other conditions, now receding into the past, they had helped people to live in a spontaneously created, but change-resistant, atrophied and corroded society: now these rules were turning into 'superstitions' and 'old wives' tales', becoming a burden and the main impediment on the road to progress and the full realization of human potential. It was therefore first and foremost necessary to deliver people from the yoke of superstitions and old beliefs, in order then to be able, through education and social reform, to fashion them according to the dictates of Reason and rationally designed social conditions.

'Education is capable of everything', said Helvetius haughtily, while Holbach would add hastily that enlightened politics would permit every citizen to enjoy a social rank given to them by birthright. In a well-organized society, the latter insisted, every class, from kings to peasants, would enjoy their very own, specific type of happiness. These fairly generalized philosophical declarations were given more practical shape by the legislators of the French Revolution, who put forward the propagation and implementation of discipline as the chief task of educators. They demanded that a regime, equal for all, would define the condition of the citizen in its every detail, and that vigilant, constant and ever-present supervision by educators would ensure the fulfilment of the obligations arising from it.[1] The role of the educators was 'culture', in the original sense of 'cultivation' borrowed from agriculture – shared by the French notion of *culture* and the simultaneously coined terms *Bildung* in Germany and *refinement* in England – terms which, although distinct in their metaphorical provenance, nevertheless captured the essential intention in a similar manner. As Philippe Bénéton concluded from an exhaustive study of commentary accompanying the implementation into everyday use of freshly coined terms,[2] at its inception the idea of 'culture' was typified by the following three characteristics: optimism, that is to say, belief that the potential for change in human nature is limitless; universalism, or an assumption that the ideal of human nature and the potential to meet its demands is the same for all nations, places and times; and finally, eurocentrism, the conviction that that ideal was discovered in Europe and that it was there that it was defined by legislators in political and social institutions, and by the ways and models of individual and communal life.

Culture was in its essence identified with Europeanization, whatever that may have meant.

The second task given to the educated classes, closely linked to the first in fact, consisted of a significant contribution to the challenge undertaken by the legislators:

to devise and build new solid structures which would determine a new rhythm of life and give shape to the momentarily 'amorphous' mass, already freed from the shackles of tradition but not yet accustomed to the new routine and disciplinary regime; in other words, to introduce a 'social order', or more precisely, to 'put society in order'.

That second task, like the first, came out of the main enterprise of the modern revolution, the simultaneous building of state and nation: the replacement of a relatively loose aggregate of local communities, with varied dialects, traditions and calendars, by a new, integrated and tightly fused whole – the 'imagined society' of a nation-state. Both tasks depended on a pooling of all the powers of the new nation-state, economic, political as well as spiritual, on the effort involved in a corporeal and spiritual remodelling of man – the chief aim and main subject of the ongoing transformation. The building of a modern nation depended on the replacement of old obligations towards one's parish, neighbourhood or guild by new civic duties towards an abstract entity independent of direct experience, and the rules it established and forcefully, or by threat of force, defended. The implementation and supervision of the new duties, as opposed to the past ones now considered to be old-fashioned, could not be entrusted to the spontaneous and somewhat instinctive and self-propelling mechanism of reproduction; they needed to be carefully and accurately designed and put into action through a process of organized mass education, with a uniform programme for all citizens. The building and administering of the modern order required managers, supervisors and teachers. The era of state and national construction demanded mutual, daily and direct engagement between managers and the managed.

Today, for a change, we are entering the epoch of non-engagement. The panoptic model of domination, with its main strategy of supervising, minutely monitoring and correcting the self-government of its subordinates, is fast being dismantled in Europe and many other parts of the contemporary world. It is giving way to self-supervision and self-control by the objects of domination, a method proving just as effective in achieving appropriate ('systematically functioning') government as the methods of domination now abandoned or marginalized – and also far less costly. Marching columns are giving way to swarms.

Swarms, as opposed to marching columns, do not require sergeants or corporals; swarms unfailingly find their way without the nosey interference of higher ranks and their daily orders. No one leads swarms to flowering meadows; no one needs to keep the members of swarms in check, preach to them, drive them on by force or threats, or keep them on course. Anyone who wishes to keep a swarm of bees on a desirable course is better off tending the flowers in the meadow, not drilling every bee in turn.

The 'ideology of the end of ideology' of multiculturalists, mentioned in the last chapter, is best interpreted as an expression of the intentions and moods of the circles described as 'culture creators' towards the 'swarm-like' human condition, shaped under the twin influences of domination by non-engagement and regulation by temptation. 'Multiculturalism', as we noted earlier, is a way of matching the place, role and tasks of the educated classes ('culture creators', one would assume, by vocation, but in practice by assignment) to these new realities. It is a manifesto of adaptation to reality: we are giving in to new realities, not questioning or undermining them – let affairs (people, their choices, and their fates consequent on those choices) 'run their own course'. It is also a mirror image of a world in which non-engagement and distance have become the chief strategy of power, and in which regulatory norms and unifying models have been replaced by a plethora of choices and excess of options. As long as these realities are not questioned, and accepted as the only unavoidable option, it may be possible to make them bearable, though only by making them into the model for one's own way of life.

In the new worldview of opinion- and culture-creators and those who accept and propagate those opinions and cultural propositions, society (invisible except to the imagination) presents itself in the form of God as seen in the late Middle Ages by the Franciscan Order (especially by one of its factions, the *fratricelli* or 'little brothers') or nominalists (especially William of Ockham). According to Michael Allen Gillespie, this Franciscan-nominalist God was 'capricious, fearsome in His power, unknowable, unpredictable, unconstrained by nature and reason and indifferent to good and evil'.[3] Above all, he obstinately remained beyond the range of human understanding and practical action. Any effort to exert pressure on God was doomed to failure; since attempts to coerce God into listening to human woes not only proved futile, but testified to blasphemous, and thus perverse and sinful, human arrogance, they were as incomprehensible as they were contemptible. As Leszek Kołakowski was later to put it, God owed nothing to the human race. Having created Man and set him on his own two feet, God commanded him to find his own path and follow it; thus He fulfilled His intention and His duty and could now distance himself from the minutiae of day-to-day supervision of human affairs. Giovanni Pico della Mirandola, codifier of the audacious ambitions of the Renaissance, in speaking of the dignity of man, drew the only conclusions he sensibly could from the fact of God's withdrawal from the management of man's daily life and from the supervision of his affairs. God, said Mirandola, made Man

> as a creature of undetermined nature, and placing him in the middle of the universe, said this to him: 'Neither an established place, nor a form belonging to you alone, nor any special function have We given to you, O Adam, and that for this reason that may have and possess, according to your desire and judgment, whatever place, whatever form, and whatever function you shall desire . . . you, who are confined by no limits, shall determine for yourself your own nature . . .'⁴

In our time it has become the turn of society (that mysterious and unknowable 'imagined being' which, by decree of the modern spirit, was to replace God in His function as administrator and supervisor of human affairs) to concur that man had been furnished with sufficient personal tools to face the challenges of life and to manage alone – and soon desisted from commandeering human choices and administering human actions.

Peter Drucker, the William of Ockham and Pico della Mirandola of the 'liquid modern' era of capitalism, summed up the principles of the new epoch with a brief but emphatic *bon mot*: 'Never again salvation by society'. Every single individual must now ensure that, having given his argument a shape consistent 'with his own will and judgement', he can prove its worth and defend it from advocates of other arguments. There is no point in deferring to the judgement of society (the last of the great authorities which the modern ear is still deemed to listen to reverently) for support of one's own choices made on one's own responsibility. First of all, not many will trust such judgements, considering that the veracity of this kind of judgement – if passed, and if there is anyone to pass them – is unknown by definition and has to remain so, since people consider 'judgements' meted out by God, Society or Fate something they learn about *ex post facto*. Secondly, what we know about popular opinion, that is to say, the judgement closest to that of 'society', is that it never remains truly popular for long, and it is not known what opinion or opinions will have replaced it by the next day. Thirdly (and perhaps most importantly), society, like the God of the late Middle Ages, is ever more clearly (in popular experience, if not in the eyes of secular theologians) 'indifferent to good and evil'.

Only when we accept that all this has indeed happened to society (or that this has been society's nature since time immemorial and has just been, belatedly, discovered and revealed) do the postulates of 'multiculturalism' begin to make sense. Since 'society' has no other preference than to leave people – individually or in partnership – to create their own preferences, there is no longer an opportunity to refer to a court which might confirm the authority or binding power of one's choices, and it is in any case impossible to establish that one preference may be better than any other. Fred Constant, commenting on the appeal formulated by

Charles Taylor for the recognition of and respect for the differences between cultures chosen by disparate communities, noted that it contained not one but two compound premises: that people have the right to be distinct, and that they also have the right to be indifferent to other people's distinctness.[5] The right to be different, and the right to be indifferent to difference – but let us note that while the right to difference is granted to others, the right to indifference (read, holding off from passing judgement and acting on it) is by and large usurped by those very people who give this right to others. When mutual tolerance combines with mutual indifference, cultural communities may live in close proximity but they will rarely speak to one another; and if they do, it will not be via the telephone but via the barrel of a gun, since any loud expostulation under these conditions is evidence of a violation of an agreement and a challenge to the status quo. A 'multicultural' world allows cultures to coexist, but the politics of 'multiculturalism' does not make it easier, indeed possibly makes it more difficult, for these cultures to gain benefits and enjoyment from their coexistence.

Constant asks whether cultural pluralism has a value in its own right, or whether it draws its value from the assumption (and hope) that it can improve the quality of existence shared by different cultures. It is not clear without further explanation which of the two multiculturalism proposes. An informed choice would first require a deeper definition of the notion of 'right to difference' – the notion is by no means unequivocal and invites at least two interpretations, each with diametrically different consequences for our inquiry.

One interpretation assumes the, so to speak,

teleological solidarity of explorers: as long as we all, singly or together, set off on a search for the best form of human coexistence and we all want to benefit from our findings, then even if we take different routes, find different possibilities along the way and come back from the expedition with different experiences and therefore different solutions, we should not deem any of them useless *a priori*, or dismiss them out of hand just because they are different from our own, inevitably preferable, solution. A variety of propositions should not cause us embarrassment: each new proposition adding to the variety should be welcome because it reduces the threat of overlooking an opportunity, or underestimating the true promise of a possibility. We ought not to assume that the value of a proposition depends on who formulated it, and on the basis of whose experience, or that we have a monopoly on finding the best solutions. This does not mean, let us make it clear, that we should accept all propositions as equally valuable and worthy of choice; inevitably, some will be better than others. It simply means that we admit to our unreadiness to give absolute opinions or pass definitive sentences. We agree that the true value and usefulness of competing propositions can only be established in the course of a multidialogue, to which all voices will be admitted, and in which all possible comparisons and juxtapositions will be made in good faith and with good intentions. In other words, the acknowledgement of cultural difference is for the sake of this argument the beginning rather than the end of the matter; the starting point of a long political process which may not be easy to see through, but which could be useful, perhaps even beneficial for all involved, and is thus a process worth undertaking.

Such a political process, expressed in a multidialogue of equal partners and aiming for an agreed and, in the longer term, shared position, would be a complete waste of time and a recipe for frustration if those conducting the debate were to assume in advance, and in their mind irrevocably, the superiority of one position over others. But the process would also come to a standstill even before it began, making no progress beyond the opening statement of faith, if it relied on the alternative interpretation of cultural difference: that is, if the participants assumed (as enthusiasts of 'multiculturalism' in its most popular contemporary version assume, whether openly or tacitly) that each existing difference deserves to survive and flourish, simply on account of its difference.

Charles Taylor quite rightly dismisses the latter interpretation, pointing out that 'true respect of equality requires more than a presumption that further study will make us see things this way, but actual judgments of equal worth applied to the customs and creations of these different cultures . . . In this form, the demand for equal recognition is unacceptable.' The question of the relative values of cultural choices, insists Taylor, should be submitted to further inquiry: 'the last thing that is expected from Eurocentric intellectuals at this stage is a positive evaluation of cultural values which have not as yet been thoroughly researched.'[6]

The acknowledgement of values, or the denial of acknowledgement, is a task for researchers, and intrinsically the prerogative, and at the same time the duty, of intellectuals, or people of learning, says Taylor. And considering the nature of academic procedure, the expectation of a mature and responsible judgement, without a prior working out and *realization* of a thorough 'research project', *sine ira et studio* – without excessive emotions either way would be as strange as it would be misleading; 'After researching the matter we will either find something highly valuable in a given culture, or we will not find it.' But it is dwellers in university study and seminar rooms who have the right, according to Taylor's conviction, to decide on the competence of research and interpret its conclusions. And so Taylor reproaches 'multiculturally' minded intellectuals for their betrayal of their academic vocation; he mentions nothing, however, about their neglect of their duty as citizens of a polity – nor does he demand that they undertake, or fulfil more eagerly than hitherto, such a duty.

When it appears to us, continues Taylor, that we know that a certain culture is inherently valuable, and as such deserves to survive, then we should have no more doubt that the difference characterizing it should be preserved for posterity, regardless of the wishes of a cultural community or the majority of its members; we ought to endeavour to limit the rights of nominal members of the community to exercise choices which would jeopardize the survival of such difference – or even deny such a right altogether. Quebec – by no means an exotic or mysterious case, but one which has been thoroughly examined and is popularly known – whose authorities oblige all inhabitants of the provinces, including English-speaking ones, to send their children to French-speaking schools, is regarded by Taylor as an example of which side and what action to take in the event of conflict:

> It is not just a matter of having the French language available to those who might choose it . . . [I]t also involves

making sure that there is a community of people here in the future that will want to avail itself of the opportunity to use the French language. Politics aimed at survival actively seek to create members of the community, for instance, in their assuring that future generations continue to identify as French-speakers.

Quebec is a 'mild' example of the conflict considered by Taylor, and it is a conflict that has so far taken place without bloodshed, imprisonment or deportation – which makes it much easier to use in support of a general thesis about the right of a community to use force for the sake of ensuring the future of a preferred culture, with the agreement, or despite the disagreement, of the people who are its members at the time. How much harder would it be to prove the truth of the proposed principle by citing other cases of friction between cultural entities, cases which, by contrast with the question of the French language (or undoubtedly any other language), would not find favour with Eurocentric, mostly multilingual intellectuals; particularly if in other, non-linguistic cases they were attached to their own likes and weaknesses and faced options that were unwanted and hard to accept, from which they would rather keep their distance, and whose assessment they might keep putting off, hiding behind the incompleteness of the research project, or the absence of a grant for undertaking it. A generalization of the Quebec conclusions would also seem to be a much more doubtful enterprise if we remember that compulsory French language education in Quebec's schools is an exceptionally unthreatening phenomenon within a wide category of cases of violence practised by communities, in one corner of the world or the other, in the name of retaining their current members and securing future ones; cases so much more dramatic and sometimes tragic in their consequences than arguments about the language of education in Quebec schools: including the requirement of female circumcision, or the prohibition against uncovering one's face in public.

The matter is undoubtedly complicated and none of the proposed solutions is without its dangers. The 'political process' already mentioned must take place under pressure from two demands that are mutually difficult or impossible to reconcile: on the one hand, we must respect the right of a community to protect its way of life from governmental pressures of assimilation and atomization; on the other hand, we should respect the individual's right of self-defence against community authorities that withhold the right to choose, or coerce the chooser into accepting unwanted or repellent options. The two imperatives are highly difficult to respect simultaneously, and we face the question on a daily basis of what to do when there is a collision between the rights of the two divided sides to protect their interests. Which of the two irreconcilable imperatives to put first, which one to sacrifice? Which, if either, has the right to denigrate the postulates of the other?

In answer to the interpretation of the cultural right to difference promoted by Charles Taylor, Jürgen Habermas introduces another value not mentioned by Taylor, the 'democratic constitutional regime'.[7] If we agree that the recognition of differences between cultures is the correct starting point for any rational discussion about the commonality of human values, then we should also agree that a 'constitutional regime' is a framework within which such a discussion can take place. To see more clearly what Habermas has in mind in insisting on the prerogatives of a 'constitutional regime', it is worth looking to the related concept of 'republic', or invoking the concept of the 'autonomous society' as formulated by Cornelius Castoriadis – remembering that an autonomous society is inconceivable without the autonomy of its members, just as a republic is unimaginable without deeply rooted and invariably respected citizens' rights. This reminder, of course, does not solve the conflict of community and individual rights, but it does highlight the fact that without the democratic practices of freely self-determining individuals, it is impossible to deal with the conflict appropriately, let alone hope to resolve it. It would be difficult to prove that the defence of the individual against the community's demand for unquestioned subordination is 'obviously' a loftier task, more worthy of praise and support, than that of the struggle of a community to retain its separate identity; but it is obvious that the defence of a citizen of a republic against communal and anti-communal violence is an elementary and irrefutable precondition of any serious undertaking of either of the two tasks. As Habermas put it:

A correctly understood theory of rights requires a politics of recognition that protects the integrity of the individual in the life contexts in which his or her identity is formed . . . All that is required is the consistent actualization of the system of rights. There will be little likelihood of this, of course, without social movements and political struggles . . . [T]he process of actualizing rights is indeed embedded in contexts that require such discourses as an important component of politics – discussion about a shared conception of good and a desired form of life that is acknowledged to be authentic.

Universality and a respect for realistic citizens' rights are the preconditions for any sensible 'policy of recognition'. It is worth adding that the universality of humanity is the benchmark against which every sensible policy of recognition must measure itself. The universality of humanity does not stand in opposition to a plurality of forms of human life: the touchstone of a truly universal humanity is its ability to accept such plurality and to make it a force for good, enabling, stimulating and maintaining an 'ongoing discussion about a common conception of welfare'. Such a test can only be passed successfully if the conditions of republican life or an 'autonomous society' are met. As Jeffrey Weeks so aptly put it, debate about common values demands 'an increase in life's opportunities and the maximization of human liberty: there is no privileged social agent to attain the ends; merely the multiplicity of local struggles against the burden of history and the various forms of domination and subordination. Contingency, not determinism, underlies our complex present.'[8]

An awareness of the unpredictable nature of fate and the uncertainty of prospects in the struggle for human community undoubtedly discourages the participants in the struggle and puts a strain on their self-confidence. But it can also mobilize them towards an ever greater effort. One of the possible responses to this uncertainty is the ideology of the 'end to all ideologies' and the practice of non-engagement; another, equally plausible, but much more promising reaction to the state of uncertainty is the conviction that the search for common humanity and the practical efforts it requires have never been as necessary or as urgent as in our epoch.

Fred Constant cites the opinion of Amin Maalouf, the Lebanese author writing in French and settled in France, about the reaction of 'ethnic minorities', that is to say immigrants, to the conflicting cultural pressures they are subjected to in the country to which they have come. Maalouf's conclusion is that the more immigrants feel that the traditions of their original culture are respected in their adopted country, and the less they are disliked, hated, rejected, frightened, discriminated against and kept at an arm's length on account of their different identity, the more appealing the cultural options of the new country appear to them, and the less tightly they hold on to their separateness. Maalouf's observations are, he suggests, of key importance to the future of inter-cultural dialogue. They confirm our previous suspicions and conjectures that there is a strict correlation between a perceived lack of threat from one side, and a 'disarm-ing' of the issue of cultural differences by the other – this as a result of overcoming impulses towards cultural separation, and a concomitant readiness to participate in the search for common humanity.

The sense of threat and uncertainty (both among immigrants and among the indigenous population) tends to turn the concept of multiculturalism into a pos-tulate of 'multicommunitarianism', as Alain Touraine, we may remember, pointed out. As a result, cultural dif-ferences, whether significant or trivial, glaring or barely perceptible, acquire the status of building materials for the construction of ramparts and rocket launch-ers. 'Culture' becomes a synonym for a fortress under siege, and the inhabitants of fortresses under siege are expected to manifest daily loyalty and give up, or at least radically curtail, any contacts with the outside world. The 'defence of the community' is given priority over any other duty. Sharing a table with 'strangers', frequenting places known as the abode and domain of outsiders, to say nothing of romances and marriages with partners from beyond the boundaries of the community, become marks of betrayal and a justification for ostracism and exile. Communities functioning on this basis become the means, first and foremost, of the greater reproduction of divisions and a deepening of separation, isolation and alienation.

A feeling of safety and the resulting self-confidence, on the other hand, are the enemies of ghetto-minded communities and the protective barriers they erect. A sense of security turns the terrifying might of the ocean separating 'us' from 'them', into an alluring and inviting swimming pool. A frightening precipice dividing a community from its neighbours gives way to a gentle plain inviting frequent walks and carefree strolls. No wonder any first signs of a dispersal of fear afflicting the community as a rule cause consternation in the advocates of communal isolation; consciously or not, they have a vested interest in the enemy missiles staying where they are, in the guns aimed at the walls protecting the community. The greater the sense of threat and the more pronounced the feeling of uncertainty it causes, the more tightly will the defenders close ranks and keep their positions, at least for the foreseeable future.

A feeling of safety on both sides of the barricade is an essential condition for a dialogue between cultures. Without it, the chance that communities will open up towards one another and start an interchange, enriching them by strengthening the human dimension of their bonds, is to say the least slim. With it, on the other hand, the prospects for humanity are rosy.

What's at stake here, is security in a much wider sense than the majority of spokespeople for 'multiculturalism' – keeping it in a tacit (or maybe unintended, even involuntary) agreement with the advocates of intercommunal separation – are prepared to admit. The narrowing of the question of general uncertainty to the real or imagined perils of two-sided cultural separateness is a dangerous mistake, drawing attention away from the roots of mutual distrust and disagreement.

First of all, people long for a sense of community today in the (mistaken) hope that it will give them shelter from the rising tide of global turmoil. That tide, however, which even the highest community breakwater cannot keep at bay, is coming from very distant places which no local powers are able to oversee, let alone control. Secondly, in our intensively 'individualizing' and 'individualized' society, human uncertainty is rooted in a deep chasm between the condition of 'individuality *de jure*' and the pressures to achieve 'individuality *de facto*'. Surrounding communities with walls will not help to breach this gulf, and it will certainly make it harder for the many community members to cross to the other side: to the status of an individual *de facto*, capable of self-determination, not just on paper. Instead of concentrating on the causes and roots of the uncertainty afflicting people today, 'multiculturalism' draws attention and energy away from them. Neither side in the ongoing wars between 'them and us' can seriously expect its long-lost and much longed-for security to return following a victory; instead, the more all of them are jointly engrossed in the planning of future clashes on the multicultural battlefield, the easier and more profitable a target they become for global powers – the only powers capable of profiting from the failure of the laborious building of human community and of joint human control of its own condition and the circumstances which shape it.

5
Culture in a uniting Europe

The European Union does not undermine the identities of the countries united in it. On the contrary, it is a champion of identity. More, it is the best insurance of its safety, offering the best likelihood of it surviving, even flourishing.

It is globalization which, by corroding the sovereignty of nation-states, is crumbling the bulwarks of territorial independence which have offered shelter to national identity and a guarantee of its safety over the last two hundred years. It would be breaking up national sovereignty even more eagerly, causing even more fractures, if it were not for the bedrock of solidarity in the European Union. The union intercepts and as far as possible neutralizes the sting of the mighty pressures reaching Europe from cyberspace, that is to say from the 'space of flows' free of political restraints. By this means, the union also safeguards nations from the potentially destructive effects of the long-standing and ongoing process (not resulting from its own initiative, and with its relatively minor and far from enthusiastic participation) of splitting apart the trinity of nation, state and territory, so inseparable for the last two hundred years. It is under the pressure of globalization, not of edicts sent out from Brussels, that the postulate and prediction formulated by Otto Bauer a century ago is coming true today: nations are turning from territorially cohesive bodies into ever more mobile and spatially dispersed associations of spiritually allied units.

It is simultaneously turning out that national cultures can well do without the (not so holy, it has to be said) trinity which was regarded as the indispensable condition of their survival during the early days of modern nation-building. According to Ernest Gellner's memorable thesis, only some of the mix of ethnic, religious and language groups which constituted Europe at the dawning of the nineteenth century had a chance to rise to the status of a nation (and so, in practice, the chance to recast in an authoritative and binding way other aspirants to nation status into ethnic minorities, other aspirants to the dignity of an official national language into dialects, and other candidates to the rank of national church into sects); yet in order to take advantage of the opportunity, nations *in spe* – in hope – needed their own, sovereign, power-wielding state . . .

Nation-building had as its goal the realization of the principle of 'one country, one nation', that is, in the last analysis, the levelling out of citizens' ethnic differences. From the perspective of a culturally united and unified nation-state, a diversity of languages or a mosaic of cultures and customs on the terrain under its jurisdiction was just the last relic, not yet quite eradicated, from times past.

Enlightening or civilizing processes presided over

and managed by the officials of the countries, already united were to ensure that those remains were not to last long. The community of the nation was after all to play a key role in legitimizing the political unification of the state, and an invocation of common roots and a common spirit was to be the main tool in an ideological mobilization to patriotic loyalty and obedience. Those postulates collided with the reality of a multicoloured mosaic of languages (now reclassified into local or tribal dialects or jargons, waiting to be replaced by one standard national/state language for all) and of traditions and customs (now reclassified as a manifestation of provincialism, parochialism or aberrant localism, awaiting replacement by a single version of common history for everyone and a common calendar of national commemorative rituals). Everything that was 'local' and 'tribal' stood for 'backwardness'; enlightenment spelled progress, and progress in turn meant an ironing out of local ways of life into a model of national culture shared by all. Within the boundaries of one state there was room for only one language, one culture, one historical memory and one loyalty.

The practice of nation-building had two faces: nationalistic and liberal. Its nationalistic face was serious and intense – usually severe, rarely gentle. Nationalism was usually combative, sometimes bloody – especially when encountering people wishing to hold on to their own habits and ill-disposed towards a 'one nation' model. Nationalism wanted to persuade and convert, but if persuasion and indoctrination failed, or if their results were slow in coming, it automatically resorted to violence: the defence of local or ethnic autonomy was deemed in conflict with the law, leaders of ethnic resistance were branded as rebels or terrorists and thrown into prison or murdered, and the use of 'dialects' in public places or situations was punished as a criminal act. The nationalistic plan of levelling out existing differences and dissolving them in a national melting pot for the sake of a one national form for all required the support of authorities. Just as the modern state needed nationalistic passions to legitimize its sovereignty and ensure civic discipline, so nationalism demanded a strong state to guarantee the success of the unification campaign. The authority demanded by nationalism was to have no rivals. All alternatives (independent of the state) were potential breeding grounds for rebellion. Self-contained, autonomous communities – ethnic or territorial – would be natural propagators of rebellious moods and havens for anti-state conspiracies.

The liberal face was altogether unlike the nationalist one. It was friendly and benevolent; as a rule smiling invitingly. It greeted coercion with contempt, cruelty with revulsion. Liberals refused to force anyone to act against their will, and most of all they did not allow anyone to do anything they themselves abhorred: they forbade both imposed conversions and the prevention, similarly by force, of conversion when it had been freely opted for by the convert. And so ethnic and local communities, even from a liberal perspective, seemed like seeds of rebellion in need of suppression or complete elimination, this time because of their natural tendency to hamper the self-sufficiency and self-definition of the individual. Liberalism believed that once enemies of liberty were deprived of liberty, and enemies of toleration were refused tolerance, then there would emerge from the dungeons of provincialism and tradition an essence common to all people. Then nothing would stand in the way of all human entities choosing for themselves, and of their own free will, one and the same loyalty and identity.

Communities saw no fundamental difference between the faces of nationalism and liberalism presented by the new nation-states: nationalism and liberalism preferred different strategies, but strived towards similar ends. There was no room for communities, certainly not autonomous and self-governing ones, in either of their plans. There was no room for them either in the nation-alist vision of 'one nation' or in the liberal model of a republic of free and unconstrained citizens. Whichever of the two faces of nation-states looked to the future, they could see only the imminent fall of the *pouvoirs intermédiaires*.

The project of nation-building gave ethnic minorities a brutal choice: assimilate or perish; in fact, to renounce their separate cultural identity willingly, or have it taken away by force. Both alternatives led to the same result: dispose of cultural differences while simultaneously getting rid of those who, for one reason or another, were not going to stop being different. The aim of the pressures to assimilate was to divest 'others' of their 'otherness': to render them indistinguishable from the rest of the nation, subsuming, digesting and dissolving their distinctiveness in the uniform amalgam of national identity. Then again the strategy of exclusion and/or of elimination of apparently indigestible and indissoluble parts of the population had a twofold function. It was used, first of all, as a means to physically or culturally separate groups or categories deemed too foreign, too deeply attached to their own customs or too resistant to change ever to lose the stigma of otherness. It was also used as a strategy of agitation: it was to awaken greater enthusiasm for assimilation among the sluggish, the unconvinced and the undecided, or to act as a push towards a meeker acceptance of their fate.

Communities were left with no choice of their fate. The decision about who was or wasn't ready for assimilation (or who should not be allowed to assimilate so as not to taint the nation and not to impair the sovereignty of the nation-state) was left to the dominant majority – that is to say, the nation which ruled the state. To dominate is tantamount to having the right and the means to change one's mind at will – and to be as a result a source of constant and incurable uncertainty for the dominated. The decisions of those in control were known to be double-edged and, even more, unpredictable. In those circumstances, every choice between the acceptance of assimilation and a categorical rejection of the offer to assimilate for the sake of holding on to one's culture at all costs was fraught with risk for the dominated minorities: the factors which made all the difference to the success or failure of their intention, or more precisely to whether it was officially approved or condemned, remained firmly beyond their control. The troubles facing the dominated were made worse by the fact that while the demand for assimilation was directed to the minority group as a whole, the responsibility for the effort to assimilate was placed firmly at the door of the individual. This duality enabled the authorities to condemn equally individuals who showed solidarity with the rest of the community struggling to assimilate, and those who turned their back on the community: in the first case they were accused of hypocrisy and disingenuousness in their conversion, in the second of an ignoble character, a readiness for personal social advancement at the expense of others.

Members of cultural minorities, as Geoff Dench has put it, 'suspended in a space between the promise of full integration and fear of the perpetual threat of banishment', could never be wholly sure whether believing themselves to be masters of their own destiny made any sense, or whether it was best to give up on official ideology and join those who were experiencing rejection.

Feelings for community arise most naturally in people at times when they are denied the right to assimilation. When they are deprived of choice, their remaining option is to seek refuge in brotherly family solidarity. The 'community' impulse of 'ethnic minorities' is not only 'natural' but imposed and driven from above, by the act or threat of dispossession: cultural minorities are deprived of the gift of the right to self-determination; their efforts to attain it are made futile. All the remaining tendencies are the consequence of that first original act of dispossession; they would not arise without it, or without the threat of it. The decision of dominant parties to contain the dominated within a framework of 'ethnic minorities', relying on their disinclination or inability to break out of it, has all the hallmarks of a self-fulfilling prophecy.

To borrow from Dench once more, the values of brotherhood are inevitably ill-disposed towards voluntarism and individual freedom. They contain no sensible conception of common human nature or of universal humanity. The only human rights they are prepared to acknowledge are those which tie up logically with obligations towards the communities which offer them.

Individual obligations do not have the character of a signed mutual agreement. Wholesale exclusion gave 'ethnic minorities' no way out so that the situation of individual members' vis-à-vis their community obligations became just as hopeless. On both levels the reaction to the spectre of banishment is the 'spirit of the besieged fortress', which devalues, or downright annihilates, all options but one: unconditional surrender to a common cause. Not only would an open refusal to accept communal duty be considered as treason; a similar verdict would fall on any perceived lack of commitment to the communal good. Any sceptical gesture, any manifestation of doubt at the wisdom of community practices would carry a whiff of a sinister, corrupt and hated 'fifth column'. In the eyes of the community, brothers who are insufficiently eager in their expression of fraternal feelings – lacking in enthusiasm, indifferent, slow to take action – find themselves regarded as 'enemy number one'. The bloodiest battles start up and are fought inside the community stronghold, not on its outer ramparts. Fraternity as a goal sanctifies fratricide as an accepted means.

Where there is wholesale exclusion of a community, no one finds leaving their community homestead easy: the rich and the capable, as much as the poor and helpless, have nowhere to go. This toughens the immunity of 'ethnic minorities' and gives them a greater chance of survival than can be relied on by other groups not fenced off from the rest of society. Those others tend to disperse, weakening their ties, and lose their identity far quicker, because of the hurried mass exodus of family elites. But the minorities of the first kind pay for their greater chances of survival with further strictures on the freedoms of their members.

There are many reasons why the strategy of building a unified nation and state has become unrealistic today. Yet more reasons combine to make the widespread practice of this strategy less urgent and less eagerly sought by governments, and downright undesirable for the public. The 'meta-reason' providing all the other reasons has to be the current form of the processes of globalization.

'Globalization' depends primarily on a network of interhuman dependencies, expanded to global dimensions. The point, however, is that this process is not accompanied by the appearance of a matching range of able and efficient institutions of political control; or anything like a truly global culture. Tightly bound up with the uneven development of the economy, politics and culture is the separation of power and politics: as power, embodied in the world distribution of capital and information, becomes exterritorial (that is external to every place), so political institutions remain, as ever before, localized. This leads inevitably to an unstoppable weakening of the nation-state; faced with inadequate means of balancing their books, or practising independent social politics, governments are in effect left with the single strategy of so-called 'deregulation': ceding control over economic and cultural processes to 'market forces', forces which are essentially exterritorial, and thus unfettered by political control.

Moving away from normative regulation, which was once the trademark of the modern state, means that the ideological-cultural mobilization of subjects, once an essential means by which it accumulated authority and power, has become redundant – just as redundant as the authorities' expectation of a civic duty of military service from its citizens. Neither one nor the other serves any obvious purpose: state authorities no longer supervise, at least not independently, the processes of social integration or system administration, those tasks for which normative regulation, the management of culture and the mobilization of patriotic sentiment were indispensable in the past. The state today prefers (by its own will or for lack of choice) to leave those tasks to forces over which it no longer has any control. Keeping order in the administered territory is the only function still remaining in the hands of state governments; states back away as fast as they can from the other functions they traditionally held, or else they share them with other powers. The fulfilment of these functions is only partly, and not independently, controlled by state powers and party organs.

This change divests the state of its former position of a superior, and by assumption and claim, the sole possessor of sovereign powers. National ambitions that once held key positions in a multidimensional sovereignty of nation-states today hang in an institutional vacuum. Any feeling of existential security falters in its foundations. Ties of blood and soil remembered from the past lose much of their former credibility in today's changed conditions. As Jeffrey Weeks repeats in another context, when old tales of group (communal) 'belonging from birth' no longer sound credible, there grows in their place a need for 'identity stories' in which 'we tell ourselves where we came from, where we are going, who we are now and where we are going'.[1] Those kinds of tales have become indispensable today for restoring a lost sense of security, for rebuilding lost confidence and, *summa summarium*, for making 'meaningful interaction with others possible'. 'As old certainties and loyalties are swept away, people seek new belongings'. However, the trouble with new narratives of identity, so decidedly different from the old tales of 'the naturalness of belonging' (a naturalness that used to be confirmed daily by the apparent stability of solidly entrenched and powerful institutions), is that 'trust and commitment have to be worked at in relationships that no one dictates should last unless individuals choose to make them last'.

The normative vacuum jointly created by globalizing and deregulating processes undoubtedly offers greater freedom to individual initiatives and actions. None of the currently told 'identity stories' are, after all, safe from revision; each can be denied at will as soon as, and for whatever reason, it ceases to please, or promises less satisfaction than the next one. It is easy to experiment in a normative vacuum free of hidden obstacles – the problem being that however pleasurable the results, they do not provide security unless they themselves consolidate into norms: their life expectancy is as short as it is undefined, and so that existential security sought through experiments, takes a long time to come. Since the only guarantee of the permanence of human bonds (among them community bonds as well) is the individual's decision that they should last, then that decision must be continuously renewed and demonstrated through an undiminishing fervour and commitment. The chosen bonds will not last if the will to keep them alive is not protested from the threat of seduction by something more solid than mere satisfaction, transient by its very nature.

This is not wholly tragic news, and it may even gladden the hearts of enterprising and capable individuals who rely on their own ability to swim against the tide and keep to their chosen course; and in the event of failure, on the possibility of a different, no less satisfying option. Such individuals do not harbour a desire for guarantees of communal security, and considering the price of any long-term obligations, do not have much enthusiasm for them either. It is different for those who are neither wealthy nor capable. For these individuals, the news that the community in which they are seeking shelter and from which they expect protection has more solid foundations than capricious and changeable personal choices is the very news they want to hear. The costs associated with involuntary, lifelong membership, never lapsing on demand, seem by no means excessive considering that the price paid of the right to free choice was – for weak and unenterprising individuals – only an illusion from beginning to end, and worse still, the cause of an unbearable complex of inadequacy and public humiliation.

For those reasons, as Jeffrey Weeks expounds,

> The strongest sense of community is in fact likely to come from those groups who find the premises of their collective existence threatened and who construct out of this a community of identity which provides a strong sense of resistance and empowerment. Seeming unable to control the social relations in which they find themselves, people shrink the world to the size of their communities and act politically on that basis. The result, too often, is an obsessive particularism as a way of embracing or coping with contingency.

Turning (quite real) individual weaknesses into the (illusory) might of a community leads to conservative ideology and the pragmatics of exclusivity. Conservatism (a 'return to roots') and exclusivism ('they' together are a threat to all of 'us') are indispensable for the word to become flesh, that is, for the imagined community to give birth to a network of dependencies which will make it and its might real; in other words, they are indispensable for W. I. Thomas's famous rule to come true, the rule which says that 'when people define situations as real, they become real in their consequences'.

As we mentioned earlier, Europe is transforming before our very eyes into a mosaic of diasporas (or more precisely into an agglomeration of overlapping and criss-crossing ethnic archipelagos). In the absence of native pressures to assimilate, it is possible to safeguard one's national identity as effectively on one of the diaspora islands as it is at home. Maybe even more effectively, since that identity, as Martin Heidegger would say, shifts in foreign lands from the domain of that which is 'given' and obvious, requiring no special care or maintenance (*zuhanden*), to the domain of that which is 'set', hence demanding action (*vorhanden*). And neighbouring, or intermixed diasporas can also mutually enrich themselves during negotiations over desired identities, and gain rather than lose power. If we are already pondering 'who and whom', let us not forget that today's (daily expanding!) Polish diaspora in the British Isles lends its Polishness to the English landscape to the same degree as it itself becomes anglicized . . .

George Steiner persuades us that the main task facing Europe today is not military or economic in nature, but rather a 'spiritual and intellectual one'.[2]

The genius of Europe is what William Blake would have called 'the holiness of the minute particular'. It is that of linguistic, cultural, social diversity, of a prodigal mosaic which often makes a trivial distance, twenty kilometres apart, a division between worlds . . . Europe will indeed perish if it does not fight for its languages, local traditions and social autonomies. If it forgets that 'God lies in the detail'.

We find similar thoughts in the literary oeuvre of Hans-George Gadamer. Among Europe's exceptional virtues, he places diversity, the wealth of variety, above all others. The abundance of diversity is deemed by him the most precious treasure Europe has managed to save from the conflagrations of the past and offer to the world today. 'To live with the Other, live as the Other's Other, is the fundamental human task – on the most lowly and the most elevated levels alike . . . Hence perhaps the particular advantage of Europe, which could and had to learn the art of living with others.'[3] In Europe, as nowhere else, 'Another' has always lived very close, within sight or within touch; metaphorically for certain, since always close in spirit, but often also literally, in a corporeal sense. In Europe, 'Another' is the closest neighbour, and so Europeans must negotiate the conditions of this neighbourhood despite the differences which divide them. The European landscape, says Gadamer, characterized as it is by 'the multilingualism, the close neighbourhood of the Other, and equal value accorded to the Other in a space tightly constrained, can be seen as a research laboratory, or a school, from which the rest of the world can carry away the knowledge and skills which determine our survival or doom'. 'Europe's task', says Gadamer, consists of passing on to all the art of everyone learning from everyone. I would add: Europe's mission, or more precisely its fate, awaits our joint effort to transform it into our own destiny.

It is impossible to underestimate the weight of this task, or the determination with which Europe should undertake it if (to echo Gadamer once more) the condition necessary, *sine qua non*, for the solution of the life problems of the contemporary world is friendship and 'cheerful solidarity'. Upon undertaking this task, we can, and should, look for inspiration to the shared European heritage: for the ancient Greeks, the word 'friend', according to Gadamer, described the 'totality of social life'. Friends are people capable and desirous of an amiable mutual relationship unconcerned by the differences between them, and keen to help one another on account of those differences; capable and willing to act with kindliness and generosity without letting go of their distinctness – at the same time taking care that that distinctness does not create a distance between them, or turn them against one another.

It follows from all of the above that all we Europeans, precisely because of the many differences between us and the differences with which we endow our shared European home in terms of the variety of our experiences and the ways of life shaped by them, are perfectly suited to become friends in the sense given to friendship by the ancient Greeks, the forefathers of Europe: not by sacrificing what is dear to our hearts, but by offering it to neighbours near and far, just as they offer us, as generously, what is dear to their hearts. Gadamer pointed out that the path to understanding leads through a 'fusion of horizons'. If that which each human agglomeration regards as truth is the basis of their collective experience, then the horizons surrounding their field of vision are also the boundaries of collective truths. If, coming from a variety of agglomerations, we wish to find and agree upon a truth common to all, we need a 'fusion of horizons', that preliminary condition of a synthesis of the experiences of separate histories but a shared future. The European Union is our chance of such a fusion. It is after all our shared laboratory, in which, consciously or not, willingly or not, we fuse group horizons, widening them all in the process. To use a different metaphor from Gadamer's: by our joint efforts and for the benefit of all, we forge out of the great variety of types of ore we bring into the laboratory an amalgam of values, ideals and intentions which may be agreeable and useful to all. If all goes well, it may display our shared values, ideals and intentions. And it just so happens, even unbeknown to us, that in the course of all this work each ore becomes finer more valuable – and we will, sooner or later, inevitably acknowledge this for ourselves.

This is protracted work, its progress slow: fast results are not to be expected. But the process could be quickened, and results achieved faster, by consciously and consistently helping the horizons to fuse. Nothing stands more in the way of fusion, and nothing slows it down as much, as the confusion of languages inherited from those who built the Tower of Babel. The European Union has acknowledged as 'official' as many as 23 languages. But in the different countries of the European Union people read, write and think in Catalan, Basque, Welsh, Breton, Gaelic, Kashubian, Lappish, Romani, a host of provincial kinds of Italian (apologies for the inevitable omissions – impossible to list them all . . .). Most of us, with the exception of a handful of extraordinary polyglots, lack access to the vast majority of

European languages. We are all impoverished and hand-icapped by this. So much inaccessible human wisdom hides in the experiences written in foreign dialects. One of the most significant, though by no means the only component of this hidden wisdom is the awareness of how astonishingly similar are the cares, hopes and expe-riences of parents, children, spouses and neighbours, bosses and subordinates, 'insiders' and 'outsiders', friends and enemies – no matter in what language they are described . . .

A pressing, if after all rhetorical question comes to mind: How much wisdom would we all have gained, how much would our coexistence, have benefited, if part of the Union's funds had been devoted to the translation of its inhabitants' writings in say, a jointly edited and published 'Library of European Culture'? Personally I am convinced that it might have been the best investment in the future of Europe and the success of its mission.

The most significant characteristic of modernity in its initial phase – its 'solid state' – was its own concep-tion of its definitive condition. This was to crown the pursuit of order, and when it was attained the changes would have run their logical and predetermined course – independent of whether the finale in view was to be a 'stable economy', a 'fully balanced system', a 'just society' or a community ruled by a codex of 'rational law and ethics'. Liquid modernity, on the other hand, releases forces that bring about changes modelled on a stock exchange or currency markets: it allows cultural mutations to 'find their own level' and from that to seek other levels; none of the current, and by definition transient levels is seen as definitive or irrevocable, and none is fixed until the game of demand and supply has run its (unpredictable) course. In keeping with the spirit of this highly effective transformation, political tricksters and cultural advocates of the 'liquid stage' of modernity, gave up almost completely on the construction of a model of social justice as the ultimate end of the planned path. The course of development is now seen as a neverending series of trials (and, undoubtedly, mistakes). Attention has shifted from ends to means; from determining the final destinations to servicing the 'journey into the unknown', from planning train routes to oiling the wheels and fuelling the locomotive. Timetables are today replaced by 'highway codes': when it comes to the future movements of history, it is the rule, standard or measure of 'human rights' which will serve as benchmark from now on in assessing successive or concurrent and competing forms of coexistence.

While in the case of models of social justice, a more or less complete list of contents was required, the principle of 'human rights' has to be limited, by its nature, to the definition of form, leaving open the question of content. The only lasting 'given' of this principle is a constant incitement to register old but as yet unsatisfied demands and articulate new ones, appealing for their recognition. It is accepted that it is impossible to foresee, or resolve once and for all, which of the many human rights and which of the many groups or categories of people demanding recognition will be or have been overlooked or ignored; which of the categories already registered were unjustly refused recognition, or were not given sufficient attention. Consecutive inventories of possible answers to this type of question are never examined thoroughly enough for any of them to be deemed complete; every collection of answers currently put forward is open to renegotiation. The provisional nature of this situation positively invites disputes and 'diagnostic clashes', or, in other words, tests of power intended to ascertain how far the opponent might allow himself to be pushed away from his chosen position, to what extent he could be persuaded to give up on one or another of his prerogatives, and what arguments might induce him to give in to demands contrary to his interests. One direct and practical consequence of the demand for recognition by invoking 'human rights' is a multiplication of battlefields and battlefronts – and a shifting of the old demarcation lines along which inherited, existing and future conflicts will gather (though, again, only for the time being).

As Jonathan Friedman suggests, we have recently found ourselves in a situation never experienced before: a world of 'modernity without modernism'.[4] As in the past, we are motivated by an eminently modern impulse to transgress, but we are no longer amused by, or even tempted to imagine, its goal or destination. That change in predilections alone can be regarded as a historical shift, yet it is not the only change. A new power elite, this time global and truly exterritorial, uninterested in or downright hostile to 'long-term obligations' (not to mention those without term, that is to say irrevocable), has abandoned the ambition of its predecessors, the nation-state elites, to establish a 'perfect order' – but it has also lost the once unquenchable appetite of the managerial elites for creating order and administering it daily. Projects for 'lofty' civilizations, sublimated cultures and the management of education in the style of

Francis Bacon's 'House of Solomon' are no longer fashionable today – and any that appear from time to time are treated on a par with other science fiction creations: if they are admired, it is only for their entertainment value, and any interest they stimulate is only temporary. As Friedman himself puts it, 'with the decline of modernism . . . only difference itself remains, and its accumulation'. There is no shortage of differences: it is not only a 'blurring of boundaries' that is taking place; 'it seems rather, that new borders appear on every corner of every new street, in every declining district of our world.'

Although the notion of 'human rights' was created for the benefit of individuals (concerning the right of every individual to be seen as separate and distinct from others, without the threat of punishment or banishment from society, or human company in general), it is obvious that the fight for 'human rights' can only be undertaken with others, since only a joint effort can secure its benefits (hence the enthusiasm mentioned above for marking out boundaries and keenly supervising of border passes). To become a 'right', a difference must be common to a sizeable group or category of individuals, rich in bargaining power; it must also be sufficiently glaring not to be ignored, to be taken seriously: the right to difference must become a stake in the joint implementation of demands.

The fight for the implementation of rights due to the individual therefore leads to an intensive building of communities: digging trenches, schooling and arming assault units, prohibiting entry to intruders and fencing off inhabitants within the confines of their settlements; in short, to a detailed examination of rights to stay and of entry and exit visas. Whenever difference is seen as a value worth fighting for and keeping at any price, there soon follows a resounding call to enlist, a popular movement and a closing of ranks, with members marching arm to arm and leg to leg. For this to happen, however, it is first necessary to find 'the difference that makes a difference' and unravel it from the mass of interhuman differences. It has to be a quality distinct and significant enough to be regarded as carrying entitlement to demands belonging to the category of 'human rights'. All in all, the principle of 'human rights' acts as a catalyst releasing the process of the construction and reproduction of difference and the building of a community around it.

Nancy Fraser protests against the 'widening gap between cultural politics of difference and the social politics of equality' and adds that 'justice demands today both recognition and redistribution':

> It is unjust that some individuals and groups are denied the status of rightful partners in social interaction, simply on the basis of institutionalized schemes of cultural values, in the building of which they did not participate on equal terms with others, and which discredit qualities which distinguish them or are attributed to them.[5]

There are clear reasons, therefore, why the logic of 'wars of recognition' provokes the warring sides to turn difference into an absolute value. Each call for recognition, after all, contains an element of a fundamentalist tendency, difficult to tone down, even harder to eliminate, usually lending the demands – in Fraser's terminology – a 'sectarian character'. The placing of the question of recognition in the context of social justice instead of the context of 'self-fulfilment' (where Charles Taylor or Axel Honneth prefer to locate it, in accordance with the currently dominant fashion for individually oriented 'culturalism') can have a beneficial effect in this domain: it can remove the venom of sectarianism (together with the poison's consequences: physical or social separation, a breakdown in communications, self-fulfilling and mutually inciting antagonisms) from the sting of demands for recognition. Since they are made in the name of equality, demands for redistribution are tools of integration, while demands for recognition reduced to the promotion of cultural differences may encourage divisions, separation and, in the end, a breakdown of dialogue.

Last, but not least, the association of 'wars of recognition' with a demand for equality may also protect the struggle for the recognition of difference from falling into the trap of relativism. Indeed, it does not follow from the definition of 'recognition' as entitlement to participation in social interaction on the basis of equality, and its consequent connection with the question of social justice, that (to quote Fraser again) 'all have equal right to social esteem' (that, in other words, all values are equal and every difference is worth cultivating by the very fact of being a difference); it merely follows that 'everyone has an equal right to demand social respect on honest terms guaranteeing equal opportunities'. The struggle for recognition, when it is squeezed into the framework of cultural self-determination and self-realization, and left there, reveals its antagonizing (and as recent experience shows, ultimately genocidal) potential. When located in the problematics of social justice, however, demands for recognition and their consequent political actions become a catalyst for encounters, dialogue and negotiations, which can (though don't have to) eventually lead to integration of a higher order – widening, not concealing the range of ethical community.

This is not about splitting philosophical hairs; what is at stake is not elegance of philosophical argument, or unity of theoretical approach – or certainly not only these things. Joining the problem of fairness of distribution to the politics of recognition adapts the modern promise of social justice to the conditions of 'liquid modernity', or, according to Jonathan Friedman, 'modernity without modernism', being, as Bruno Latour suggests,[6] an epoch of agreement to the permanent coexistence of diversity – that is, a condition which more than any other demands the art of peaceful human cohabitation.

'Modernity without modernism' is also a condition in which it is no longer feasible to hope for a radical rooting out of human misery and liberation of the human condition from conflict and suffering, once and for all. If the idea of the 'good society' is to remain meaningful in the landscape of liquid modernity, it must stand for a society dedicated to the idea of 'giving everyone a chance', that is, to removing one by one the obstacles preventing those chances from being fulfilled. We know that those obstacles cannot be removed wholesale, in one fell swoop, by the imposition of another mode of order; therefore the only possible strategy of a 'just society' is a gradual elimination of obstacles as they appear with each consecutive call for recognition. Not every difference has the same value, and some lifestyles and forms of communality are ethically more praiseworthy than others; we won't find out which is which, however, if both sides are not given equal rights to present their arguments and prove their points. It is impossible, by the very nature of an honest dialogue, to prejudge what ways of life might emerge in the course of negotiations; conclusions cannot be drawn from the desiderata of philosophical logic.

'In reality', as Cornelius Castoriadis stressed, 'no problem can be solved in advance. We must create good in uncertain and ill-defined conditions. The project of autonomy is a goal, a pointer, it will not solve real problems for us.'[7] We can only say that the right to call for recognition and to receive society's response is an indispensable, and possibly even decisive condition of autonomy, that is, the ability to self-constitute (thus potentially 'self-perfect') the society we live in; and that it gives us the possibility that no injustice and no trouble will be concealed, overlooked or ignored, and that they will not be prevented in any other way from taking their rightful place among the problems demanding solution. As Castoriadis himself pointed out: 'the whole matter begins and ends with the relocation of social activity – which, if given a chance, would leave far behind everything we are capable of thinking today . . .' The 'sensible persuasion' of people today means helping them to attain their autonomy.

Castoriadis clearly stipulates that he 'does not respect others' differences for their own sake, regardless of who they are and what they do'. The recognition of 'human rights', the right to recognition, is not tantamount to signing a blank cheque and does not signify *a priori* agreement to the way of life which was, is or is going to be the subject of demands. The recognition of such rights is nothing more and nothing less than an invitation to a dialogue, in the course of which the merits and defects of the differences under consideration can be discussed and (with any luck) an agreement on their recognition can be reached. Such an attitude is radically different from that of universal fundamentalism, which rejects all other forms of 'being human', while granting only one form the right to an uncontested existence; but it is just as radically different from a specific kind of tolerance propagated by some strains of the so-called politics of 'multiculturalism', which assumes an essentialist character of difference, thus refusing from the outset any negotiations between different lifestyles. Castoriadis's viewpoint demands that culture be defended on two fronts; on one side from *Kulturkampf* – cultural crusades and oppressive homogenization – and on the other, from the high-handed and soulless indifference of non-engagement.

6

Culture between state and market

French state involvement in the arts began earlier than in most European countries, under royal and aristo-cratic patronage. Francis I even established a state workshop in the sixteenth century for the production of tapestries. More than a hundred years later Louis XIV (famous for saying 'the state is me') made a decisive step in the direction of modern forms of state art patronage by founding the royal theatre, the Comédie-Française, as well as a number of royal academies (including of music and painting) to develop the arts and educate the artists.

Early arts funding by authorities, and initiatives which would today come under the title of 'cultural policy', appeared a good two hundred years before the term 'culture' was first coined: we may surmise that the concept grew out of royal ambition and enterprise. The French concept of *culture* arose as a collective name for the government's efforts to promote learning, soften and improve manners, refine artistic tastes and awaken spiritual needs the public had not hitherto possessed, or were not aware they possessed. 'Culture' was something that some people (the educated and powerful elite) did, or intended to do, for other people ('people' or 'common people', in both cases deprived of education and power). French 'culture' was a somewhat messianic notion in its early days – it signalled proselytizing intentions: enlightening, eye-opening, converting, refining, perfecting. This messianic vocation was appropriated by, or perhaps entrusted to the state authorities from the first.

After the abolition of the French monarchy, the revolutionary government seized the mission, filling the idea of enlightenment and culture with ambitions that had not occurred to the dynastic rulers. The purpose of the mission now became the rebuilding of society 'from its foundations', the creation of the 'new man', rescuing of the 'people' from the abyss of centuries of ignorance and superstition – in short the implementation of a new, elaborately and carefully worked out model of society and the individual. If it was possible to abolish the monarchy and its aristocratic hangers-on everything was possible, everything could be reworked and turned inside out; all that was needed was to know what to do and how to go about it. The concept of 'culture' became a call to action and a battle cry.

Between 1815 and 1875 the state regime changed five times, but with all the drastic differences dividing one from another, one matter established by their predecessors was accepted unquestioningly by all: the necessity for state authorities to continue with their support and supervision of efforts to enlighten and cultivate, now known collectively as the 'development and dissemination of culture'. In this period, too, the tradition already established of state responsibility for culture was enlisted into the service of nation-building. The general aim of creating new (and better) individuals turned specifically into the task of creating French patriots and loyal citizens of the Republic. The concept of *patrimoine*, the national heritage – to be cared for and made accessible to the citizen (and further enriched for the good and glory of future inheritors), being deemed, quite rightly, one of the greatest conditions of identity, national unity and citizen loyalty and discipline, took an ever more significant place in the consecutive programmes of the enterprise. It was through an integrated cultural programme that the conglomeration of local traditions, customs, dialects and calendars inherited from centuries of feudal fragmentation was to be unified into a modern state.

A number of relatively sporadic and brief attempts to institutionalize and codify the state's curatorship of cultural activity had taken place in the past, but it wasn't until 3 February 1959, during the presidency of Charles de Gaulle in the Fifth Republic, that a Ministry of Cultural Affairs was established, seemingly permanently. De Gaulle appointed André Malraux as its first minister, and it was he who achieved what had been undertaken many times before with only minor and transitory success. The political situation in the country at the time was favourable to the enterprise: the leader of the country, dedicated to the mission of reviving France's impaired wartime position in Europe, wished for culture to be part of his country's future glory, and that French culture should radiate over the rest of the continent, becoming its admired and much copied model. Culture was to bestow prestige and glory worldwide on the country under whose patronage it thrived. As François Chabot put it over half a century later, in an article on the diffusion of French culture in the world,[1] the task of promulgating French culture worldwide, undertaken (though not necessarily accomplished) by state art patronage, 'remains the subject of acute national concern, since few other factors are as deeply influential on the way a country is perceived by the world, and on its ability to speak and be heard . . .'

According to Chabot, the attitude to art of successive French governments was shaped by ideas of 'political-cultural messianism', although the concept of the mission undertaken by France changed over time (in the nineteenth century it was concerned mainly with the right of nations to self-determination, in the interwar period with the defence of the still fragile and insecure democracies, and at the end of the twentieth century with the promotion of multiculturalism). The Minister of Culture therefore, had no shortage of additional funds with which to illustrate the benefits resulting from state guardianship for artists, cultural workers and those profiting from their efforts. 'Culture' was now understood mainly as art and artistic creation, and the multiplication of the former and the intensification of the latter became the focus of the newly established ministry's activities; political democracy was to be complemented by the democratization of art. Malraux himself formulated the task as follows: 'The ministry entrusted with cultural affairs has a mission to make accessible the greatest works of humanity, especially the French, to the greatest number of Frenchmen; a mission to ensure the greatest possible audience for our cultural heritage and to promote works of art which enrich that legacy.'

99

Malraux emphatically rejected any tasks of a pedagogical nature, in particular ideas of forcing artistic choices or general canons of cultural preference on the nation. Unlike his predecessors, he was not interested in imposing models or tastes worked out 'at the top', chosen by authorities above the heads of the 'objects of cultivation' and foisted on them, or in implementing preferred content and forms into workshops and artists' ateliers. He was more interested in creating opportunities: for creators, opportunities to create; for artists, opportunities to refine their art; for all others, the opportunity to associate intimately with both (Malraux spoke of putting culture 'at the disposal of all, not in the service of decorating bourgeois lives').

Malraux's successors followed the route he had designated – and the logic of the development of the information society, in conjunction with the logic of the principles formulated and tested by the first minister of culture, directed that path inexorably towards recognition of a multiplicity of cultural choices, and eventually to the adoption of cultural pluralism as the main peculiarity, and a title to glory, of French culture, supported and strengthened by state patronage as its main goal. The cultural policies of successive governments, both right-wing and left-wing, would have been perfectly served by Mao's motto 'Let a hundred flowers bloom' had it not turned out that this apparently hospitable and essentially liberal invitation was a trap insidiously set for Chinese creators to persuade them to disclose their secret heretical intentions in order to nip them in the bud . . . In France the motto of cultural plurality and artistic diversity was to remain a beacon for cultural politics with a praiseworthy constancy. President

Georges Pompidou dotted the i, stating emphatically that 'art is not an administrative category, but is, or should be the framework [*cadre*] of life'.

The practice of supporting cultural pluralism reached its peak during the presidency of François Mitterrand, with Jack Lang as minister. In a decree of 10 May 1982 inspired by Mitterrand and written by Lang, it was declared that the fundamental mission of the Ministry of Culture should be to enable all the French to foster their innovation and creativity, develop their own creative powers, freely demonstrate their talents and benefit from the artistic training of their own choice. In order to achieve this objective, the decree imposed on state institutions the duty to support regional and group initiatives, and to assist independent and non-institutionalized movements and amateur practices. The development of art, its wealth, prevalence and availability, as Lang tirelessly and obsessively stressed over time, demands a decisive decentralization of cultural initiatives. The powers, funds and organizational know-how of the Ministry of Culture were not there to steer cultural trends and choose between them, but to increase the powers and fund the self-organization of spontaneously emerging regional initiatives. Mark Fumaroli, a member of the French Academy and author of a sharply polemical, widely acclaimed and fiercely debated tract about the historical intricacies of 'l'état culturel', the cultural state, commented somewhat bitingly that the main concern of the French Ministry of Culture was to avoid suspicion of its intentions to govern culture and accusations of favouring one of its variants. Fumaroli by no means considered such a stance admirable. Yet, on another hand, Theodor Adorno, known for his suspicions of the motives of state administrations when they took an interest in the arts, would probably greet with favour the withdrawal of the administration from its old ambitions to judge the merits and demerits of artistic proposals.

Theodor Adorno notes that embodying the objective spirit of an epoch in a single concept of 'culture', instantly betrays an administrative viewpoint; from its higher perspective, the task is one of collating, distributing, valuing and organizing – and he goes on to list the characteristic of that viewpoint:

> The demand made by administration on culture is essentially heteronomous: culture – no matter what form it takes – is to be measured by norms not inherent to it, and which have nothing to do with the quality of the object, but rather with some type of abstract standards imposed from without.[2]

But, as is to be expected from such an asymmetrical social relationship, an altogether different sight will greet the eyes of those who experience this state of affairs from the opposite end – from the side of the managed, not the managers; and an altogether different conclusion would be drawn if those observers were permitted to pass judgement. We would then expect to be shown a panorama of unfounded and unwanted repression, and a verdict of injustice and lawlessness. From that other perspective, culture appears in opposition to management, and that is so because, as Oscar Wilde put it (provocatively, according to Adorno), culture is 'useless', or at least seen to be such, so long as the (self-appointed, and from art's point of view illegal) supervisors have a monopoly on laying down the boundary lines between usefulness and uselessness. In this sense, according to Adorno, 'culture' represents the interests and demands of the particular as against the homogenizing pressures of the 'general' – and takes on an uncompromisingly critical stance towards the existing state of affairs, and its institutions.[3]

Collisions and a constantly simmering antagonism between two perspectives and narratives deriving from different experiences cannot be avoided. It is impossible to prevent conflicts from emerging and it is also impossible to stem the antagonism once it happens. The relationship between management and the managed is antagonistic by nature: the two sides aspire to opposite outcomes and can only exist in a state of potential collision, in an atmosphere of mutual distrust and under pressure from an ever growing temptation to pick a fight.

The conflict is especially glaring, the clashes particularly bitter and relations singularly fraught with catastrophic consequences in the case of the fine arts – the foremost area of culture and the powerhouse of its dynamics. The fine arts are the most hyped up area of culture; for that reason they cannot resist making ever new forays into fresh territory and waging guerrilla warfare in order to forge, pave and plot ever new pathways to be followed by the rest of human culture ('art is not a better, but an alternative existence', noted Joseph Brodsky, 'it is not an attempt to escape from reality, but the opposite: an attempt to animate it').[4] Creators of art are by their very nature adversaries or competitors in activities which managers would, after all, prefer to make into their own prerogatives.

The more they distance themselves from the existing

order and the more staunchly they refuse to give in to it, the less suited are the arts and artists to the tasks placed on them by the administration; this in turn means that their managers will regard them as useless, if not downright harmful to the enterprise. Managers and artists present one another with opposite aims: the spirit of management remains in a state of constant warfare with the contingency which is the natural territory/ecotype of art. But, as we noted a moment ago, the preoccupation of the arts with sketching in imaginary alternatives to the prevailing state of things sets them up as rivals to the management whether they like it or not. The control over human enterprise and effort expended by the administration comes down in the last resort, to its desire to dominate the future. There are therefore plenty of reasons why there should be no love lost between administrators and people in the arts.

Speaking of culture, but mostly bearing in mind the fine arts, Adorno acknowledges the inevitability of conflict with the administration. But he also claims that the antagonists need one another; and, what is more, art needs champions, resourceful ones at that, since without their help, its vocation cannot be fulfilled. It is a situation not unlike that in many marriages where spouses are unable to live together in harmony, yet they cannot live apart from each other either; however uncomfortable, unpleasant and unbearable a life full of open clashes and argument, a life poisoned daily by a hidden mutual hostility may be, there is no greater misfortune that could befall culture (or more precisely the fine arts) than its complete and unconditional triumph over its opponent: 'Culture suffers damage when it is planned and administered; yet when left to itself, everything cultural threatens not only to lose its possibility to have an effect, but its very existence as well.'[5] In expressing this view Adorno once again draws the doleful conclusion he reached with Max Horkheimer while working on the *Dialectic of Enlightenment*: that the history of old religions, as well as the experience of modern parties and revolutions, teach us that the price of survival is the 'transformation of the idea into domination'.[6] This history lesson needs to be assiduously studied, says Adorno, in order for it, to be assimilated and impressed upon the practices of professional artists, who carry the main burden of the 'transgressive' function of culture, and consciously accept responsibility for it, thereby making criticism and transgression into a way of life:

> The appeal to the creators of culture to withdraw from the process of administration and keep distant from it has a hollow ring. Not only would this deprive them of the possibility of earning a living, but also of every effect, every contact between work of art and society, something which the work of greatest integrity cannot do without, if it is not to perish.[7]

What can one say: this is indeed a paradox and one of the hardest to solve at that . . . Managers must defend the order entrusted to their care as the 'order of things', that is to say, the very system that artists loyal to their vocation must tax, thereby exposing the perversity of its logic and questioning its wisdom. As Adorno suggests, administration's innate suspiciousness towards the natural insubordination and unpredictability of art cannot but be a constant *casus belli* for artists; on the other hand, as he does not fail to add, creators of culture cannot get through without administration if, loyal to their vocation and wishing to change the world (for the better if at all possible), they want to be heard and seen, and as far as possible, heard out and noticed. The creators of culture have no choice, says Adorno: they must live with this paradox on a daily basis. However loudly artists may curse the contentions and interventions of the administration, the alternative to a modus covivendi is a loss of meaning in society and an immersion in non-being. Creators can choose between more or less bearable forms and styles of management, but they cannot choose between acceptance and rejection of the institution of management as such. Having the right to such a choice is an unrealistic dream.

The paradox discussed here cannot be solved because, despite all the conflicts between them and silent or noisy mud-slinging, cultural creators and officials cohabit in the same household and participate in the same enterprise. Their disputes are a manifestation of what psychologists would describe as 'sibling rivalry'. Both one and the other are governed by the same understanding of their role and its purpose in a shared world, which is to make that world different from what it would continue to be, or become, without their intervention and input into its condition and functioning. Both of them harbour a (not unfounded) doubt as to the ability of the existing or desired order to sustain itself, or to come into being by its own powers and without their help. They do not disagree that the world needs a constantly vigilant monitoring and frequent adjustment; the disagreement concerns the subject of adjustments and the direction the corrections should take. At the last count, the only stake in the argument and constant power struggle is the right to make decisions on the matter, and then to make one's point stand and one's decision binding.

Hannah Arendt went a step further and looked beyond the direct stake in the conflict, reaching so to speak, to the existential roots of discord:

> An object is cultural depending on the duration of its permanence: its durable character is opposed to its functional aspect, that aspect which would make it disappear from phenomenal world through use and wear and tear. . . . Culture finds itself under threat when all objects of the world, produced currently or in the past, are treated solely as functions of the vital social processes – as if they had no other reason but satisfaction of some need – and it does not matter whether the needs in question are elevated or base.[8]

According to Arendt, culture reaches beyond and above current realities. It is not concerned with what might be the order of the day at a given point, what might be hailed as 'the imperative of the moment'; it strives not to be bound by limits defined by the 'actuality' of the matter – whoever might have declared it as such and by whatever means they did so – and to free itself from the constraints it imposes.

To be used and consumed on the spot, or moreover to be damaged in the course of use and consumption, is not, according to Arendt, what cultural products are destined for, and nor is it the measure of their worth. Arendt claims that the point of culture (i.e. art) is beauty. I think she chooses to define the interests of culture in this way because the idea of beauty is a synonym or embodiment of an ideal which resolutely and stubbornly eludes rational justification or causal explanation; beauty by its nature is devoid of purpose or obvious use, it serves nothing but itself – and nor can it justify its existence by invoking a recognized, palpable and documented need which impatiently and noisily demands to be satisfied. Whatever needs art might eventually satisfy, they must first be conjured up and brought to life by the act of artistic creation. A thing is 'a cultural object' if it lasts longer than whatever practical use might accompany or inspire its creation.

Cultural creators may rebel today, as they did in the past, against a meddling and intrusive intervention which insists on assessing cultural objects according to criteria which are alien and ill-disposed to the natural non-functionality, unruly spontaneity and intractable independence of creation; they may rebel against bosses, both appointed and self-appointed, who exploit the powers and means at their disposal to demand compliance to rules and standards of usefulness they themselves have drawn up and defined; who, *summa summarum*, just as in the past, clip the wings of artistic imagination and undermine the principles of artistic creation. And yet something has changed in the last few decades in the situation of art and its creators: first, the nature of the managers and administrators currently in charge of art, or aspiring to that position; secondly, the means they use to achieve it; third, the sense given by the new breed of managers to the notion of the 'functionality' and 'usefulness' they expect of art and which they use to tempt it and/or make demands on it.

Andy Warhol, with his customary taste for paradox and contradiction and with an ear remarkably attuned to the latest trends, asserted in one breath that an 'artist is someone who makes things that no one needs', and that 'being good in business is the most fascinating kind of art. Making money is art and working is art and good business is the best art.' The temptation offered by heads of operations of the consumer market – specialists, in other words, in increasing demand in step with supply – consists of a promise that under the new management those two statements will no longer be contradictory: the new bosses will ensure that people feel the need to possess (and pay for) precisely what artists want to create, and that the practice of art will become 'good business'. The coercion, on the other hand, consists of the fact that from now on the will of the new authorities will dictate which artistic creations there will be demand for and which kind of creativity will become 'good business', that best art of all – an art at which art marketing experts beat masters of the brush or the chisel hands down.

Mediation in the bringing of art to the public is nothing new: it used to be, for better or worse, in the hands of state patronage, bringing artists greater or lesser satisfaction; it was dealt with by the political institutions responsible for culture. What is truly new are the criteria used in this mediation by the new breed of managers, agents of market forces, claiming the positions abandoned by (or taken away from) the agents of state authorities. As these are criteria of market consumption, they are mostly concerned with issues such as immediacy of consumption, immediacy of gratification and immediacy of profit. A consumer market working to satisfy long-term needs, to say nothing of needs that are everlasting or timeless, is a contradiction in terms, an oxymoron. The consumer market favours and promotes a quick turnover and the shortest possible time interval between use and disposal – for the sake of providing immediate replacements for goods that are no longer profitable. Such a stance, typical of the 'spirit of our times', which according to Milan Kundera 'stares into what is now, into a present so all-conquering and so expansive that it pushes the past out of our range of vision, and brings time into one ever-present moment',[9] exists in sharp contradiction to the nature of artistic creation and the purpose of all art, not only the novel of which Kundera speaks. The mission of art, to quote Kundera once more, is to 'safeguard us from forgetting to be'. What is new, therefore, with reference to previous observations, is a parting of the ways for the siblings still engaged in mutual rivalry.

What is at stake in today's phase of the age-old push and shove is not only the answer to the question 'who is in charge', but the very sense of managing art, the purpose of management and its desired consequences. We could go further and presume that what is at stake is the survival of the arts in the form in which they existed from the times when the walls of the caves in Altamira were covered in drawings. To subject cultural activity to the standards and criteria of consumer markets is tantamount to a demand for works of art to accept the entry conditions placed before any products aspiring to the rank of consumer goods – that is to justify themselves in terms of their current market value. But can culture survive the devaluation of being and the decline of eternity, possibly the most painful kinds of collateral damage caused by the triumph of consumer markets? We do not know, and we cannot know the answer to this question yet – and so we could do worse than to heed the sensible advice of the philosopher Hans Jonas, to trust more, when times are uncertain, the dark predictions of the 'prophets of doom' than the placatory assurances of the promoters and fans of the 'wonderful new world of consumers'.

The first question asked of new art initiatives looking for recognition is about their prospects for market demand supported by financial means of potential buyers. Let us remember, however, that consumerist intentions are notoriously capricious and transitory, and that the story of the domination of art by consumer markets is therefore studded with false prognoses and mistaken and misleading assessments, and the wrong decisions stemming from them. The logic of this domination comes down in practice to a compensation for a lack of aesthetic criteria of quality by a multiplication of offers, 'stacking the shelves high', or, to put it simply, wasteful excess and excessive waste. George Bernard Shaw, not only great playwright but also a keen lover of photography, used to advise his fellow amateurs that in taking photographs they should follow the example of the cod, which has to lay thousands of eggs so that just one of the baby fishes will be able to live till maturity; it seems that the whole of the consumer industry and its marketing agents have taken to heart more than most the warnings and advice of George Bernard Shaw.

It is potential clients, or more precisely their number, the contents of their bank accounts and the size of the credit available to them, that decide today, consciously or not the fate of cultural products. The line dividing 'successful' art (read, art catching the public's attention) from unsuccessful, poor or ineffective art (read, the art which did not manage to get through to well-known galleries or auction houses frequented by the right clientele) is drawn with reference to sales statistics, frequency of exposure and profits. As with the partly, but not wholly, ironic definition by Daniel J. Boorstin, 'Celebrities are people who are famous for being famous', 'a good book is the book which sells well, because it is very sellable'. Theoreticians and art critics assessing the worth of works of art coming onto the market today, and attempting to find a correlation between the popularity of an artist and the worth of his or her work of art, have managed to get no further, or dig no deeper, than Boorstin did with his witticisms. When looking for a decisive reason for an artist's high prices, it is easier to find it in the name of the gallery, television show or newspaper responsible for getting the artist and the work out of the shadows and into the glare of publicity, than in the works of art themselves.

It is not only institutions and businesses that add value to works of art by supplying them with their brand, or devalue them by withdrawing it; the bestowing of an 'imprimatur' is accompanied by an event, one-off and short-lived, but loudly 'heralded', a multimedia bacchanalian event of 'hype' or 'promotion'. Events now appear to be the richest source of culture's added value. In keeping with Boorstin's recipe, they attract the attention of the masses because the masses pay attention to them, and they sell vast numbers of tickets because there are long queues for those tickets. . .

Events are free of the risks to which even the most famous galleries and auditoria are exposed. They have the advantage that in a world attuned to the capriciousness, fragility and transience of public memory, and in the presence of countless desirable and tempting attractions competing for access to chronically depleted attention, they don't need to count on the – under the circumstances doubtful – loyalty of faithful clients: events, as well as all other bona fide consumer products, are fitted with a (usually very short) sell-by date. Their designers and operators can therefore remove long-term worries from their calculations, thereby curbing their expenses – and, what is more, gain in credibility and prestige thanks to a perceived resonance between their character and the spirit of the times. Events, according to George Steiner, are designed for maximal impact and instant obsolescence, and they thereby avoid the plague of any long term investment, which is the 'law of diminishing returns', known in practice to every farmer in history, and in theory to every economist since Turgot, Malthus and Ricardo.

The overwhelming race of events, of activities never lasting longer than the average life-span of the public's interest, the richest source of market revenue today, harmonizes perfectly with a tendency popular in the liquid modern world. The products of culture are created these days with 'projects' in mind, projects with a predetermined, and most frequently the shortest possible, lifespan. As Naomi Klein has noticed, firms which prefer to earn their revenue by sticking their own labels onto readymade products, rather than accepting responsibility for their production and all the risks this entails, can make anything into the subject of this procedure: 'not only sand, but wheat, beef, bricks, metals, concrete, chemicals, millet and an endless variety of goods traditionally regarded as immune to such forces'[10] – goods, in other words, which were deemed (erroneously as it turned out) to be able to prove their worth and useful-ness thanks to their own, easily provable qualities and virtues. The absence of works of art from this list must be put down to a rare case of Naomi Klein's oversight . . .

For centuries, culture existed in an uneasy symbio-sis with all sorts of wealthy patrons and impresarios, towards whom it had very mixed feelings, and in whose self-appointed embrace it felt restricted, indeed stifled – while often cooling its temper with them by frequent requests or demands for help, and returning from many an audience with new vigour and fresh ambitions. Will culture benefit or lose from the 'change of manage-ment'? Will it come out in one piece after the change of guards in the watchtower? Will it survive that change? Will its works of art enjoy more than the chance of a fleeting life and fifteen minutes of fame? Will the new administrators, in keeping with today's fashionable style of management, not limit their custodial activities to 'asset stripping', taking away their charges' assets and keeping them? Will the 'cemetery of cultural events' not replace the 'mountain rising skyward', to use the most suitable metaphor for the state culture is in? We need to wait a little longer for the answers to these ques-tions. But we must not put off searching for them, and energetically at that. Nor must we neglect the question of what shape culture will finally take as a result of our actions or lack of them.

State patronage of national culture has not been saved from the fate of many other 'deregulated' and 'priva-tized' functions of the state – like them, and for the sake of the market, it has willingly jettisoned ever more tasks which it could no longer hold in its weakening grasp.

But there are two functions it is impossible to deregulate, privatize and cede without socially catastrophic 'collateral damage'. One is the function of defending markets from themselves, from the consequences of their notorious incapacity for self-limitation and self-control, and their equally notorious tendency to belittle all values resistant to valuation and negotiation, dropping them from their list of planned actions, and the cost of doing so from calculations of cost-effectiveness. The other is the function of repairing the social and cultural damage which litters the trail of market expansion because of this incapacity and tendency. Jack Lang knew what he was doing . . .

I could not sum up these considerations and draw practical conclusions from them better than Anna Zeidler-Janiszewska, insightful researcher into the fate of artistic culture in the post-war Europe:

> If we differentiate artistic culture (as 'mental reality') from the practice of participation in it (creative and receptive participation – more so today: creative-receptive or receptive-creative participation), and the institutions that make that participation possible, then a state cultural policy should concern itself with institutions of participation (which include 'public' media), and its primary concern is to equalize opportunities for participation . . . The quality of and equal opportunities for participation, in other words 'recipients' rather than content and form, or relations between the 'managers' and the 'public of arts' are the focal point of cultural policy.[11]

It follows from our previous considerations that the cultural creations and the cultural choices and uses made of them by their 'recipients' are locked in intimate interaction – nowadays more than at any period in the past; and that, given the changing location of arts in the totality of contemporary life, this interaction is in all probability bound to grow still tighter in the future. Indeed, contemporary works of art tend to be under-determined, underdefined, incomplete, still in search of their meaning and as yet unsure of their potential – and bound to remain so until the moment of their encounter with their 'public' (more exactly, the 'public' they invoke and/or provoke and thereby bring into being), an encounter active on both sides; the true meaning (and therefore the enlightening and the change-promoting potential) of the arts is conceived and matures within such an encounter. The best among the contemporary arts (indeed the most seminal and the most effective in the performance of their cultural role) are ultimately so many steps in an unending process of reinterpreting shared experience, and offer standing invitations to a dialogue – or, for that matter, a perpetually widening polylogue.

Just as the true function of the capitalist state in administering the 'society of producers' used to be to secure a continuous and fruitful encounter between capital and labour, while the true function of the state presiding over the 'society of consumers' is to secure frequent and successful encounters between consumer products and the consumer, so the focus of the 'cultural state', a state bent on the promotion of the arts, needs to focus on securing and servicing the continuous encounter between the artists and their 'public'. It is in this kind of encounter that the arts of our times are conceived, begotten, stimulated and fulfilled. It is for the sake of such an encounter that local, 'grassroots' artistic and performative initiatives need to be encouraged and supported: like so many other functions of contemporary state, the sponsorship of cultural creativity urgently waits to be 'subsidiarized'.

Notes

Chapter 1

1 Richard A. Peterson, 'Changing arts audiences: capitalizing on omnivorousness', workshop paper, Cultural Policy Center, University of Chicago, at http://culturalpolicy.uchicago.edu/papers/working papers/peterson1005.pdf (accessed December 2010).
2 Pierre Bourdieu, *Distinction: A Social Critique of the Judgement of Taste*, Routledge Classics, 2010.
3 Oscar Wilde, *The Picture of Dorian Gray*, Penguin Classics, 2003.
4 Sigmund Freud, *Civilisation, Society and Religion*, Penguin Freud Library vol. 12, 1991, p. 271.
5 Philip French, 'A Hootenanny New Year to all', *Observer Television*, 30 Dec. 2007–5 Jan. 2008.

Chapter 2

1 Georg Simmel, *Zur Psychologie der Mode; Soziologische Studie*, in Simmel, *Gesamtausgabe*, vol. 5, Suhrkamp, 1992.

2 Sławomir Mrożek, *Małe listy*, Noir sur Blanc, 2000, p. 121.

3 Ibid., p. 273.

4 Ibid., p. 123.

5 Quotations from Blaise Pascal, *Pensées*, trans. A. J. Krailsheimer, Penguin, 1966, p. 68.

Chapter 3

1 Jonathan Rutherford, *After Identity*, Laurence & Wishart, 2007, pp. 59–60.

2 Saskia Sassen, 'The excesses of globalisation and the feminisation of survival', *Parallax* 7(1) (Jan. 2001): 100–1.

3 Geoff Dench, *Maltese in London: A Case Study in the Erosion of Ethnic Consciousness*, Routledge & Kegan Paul, 1975, pp. 158–9.

4 Richard Rorty, *Achieving our Country: Leftist Thought in 20th Century America*, Harvard University Press, 1998, p. 88.

5 Alain Touraine, 'Faux et vrais problèmes', in Michel Wieviorka, ed., *Une société fragmenté. Le multiculturalisme en débat*, La Découverte, 1997.

6 See Russell Jacoby, *The End of Utopia: Politics and Culture in an Age of Apathy*, Basic Books, 1999.

Chapter 4

1 See Bronislaw Baczko, ed., *Une éducation pour la démocratie*, Garnier Frères, 1982, pp. 377ff.

2 See Philippe Bénéton, *Histoire de mots – culture et civilisation*, Presses de Sciences Po, 1975, pp. 23ff.

3 Michael Allen Gillespie, 'The theological origins of modernity', *Critical Review* 13(1–2) (1999): 1–30.

4 Giovanni Pico della Mirandola, *Oration on the Dignity of Man*, trans L. Kuczynski, in *Przeglad Tomistyczny* vol. 5, 1995, p. 156.
5 Fred Constant, *Le multiculturalisme*, Flammarion, 2000, pp. 89–94.
6 Charles Taylor, 'The policy of recognition', in Amy Gutmann, ed., *Multiculturalism*, Princeton University Press, 1994, pp. 98–9, 88–9.
7 Jürgen Habermas, 'Struggles for recognition in the democratic constitutional regime', in Amy Gutmann, ed., *Multiculturalism*, Princeton University Press, 1994, pp. 125, 113.
8 Jeffrey Weeks, 'Rediscovering values', in Judith Squires, ed., *Principled Positions*, Lawrence & Wishart, 1993, pp. 208–9.

Chapter 5
1 Jeffrey Weeks, *Making Sexual History*, Polity, 2000, pp. 182, 240–3.
2 George Steiner, *The Idea of Europe*, Nexus Institute, 2004, pp. 32–4.
3 See Hans-Georg Gadamer, *Das Erbe Europas*, Suhrkamp, 1998.
4 Jonathan Friedman, 'The hybridization of roots and the abhorrence of the bush', in M. Featherstone and S. Lash, eds, *Spaces of Culture*, Sage, 1999, pp. 239, 241.
5 Nancy Fraser, 'Social justice in the age of identity politics: redistribution, recognition and participation', in D. Clausen and M. Werz, eds, *Kritische Theorie der Gegenwart*, Institut für Soziologie der Universität Hannover, 1999, pp. 37–60.

6 See Bruno Latour, 'Ein Ding ist ein Thing', *Concepts and Transformations* 1–2 (1988): 97–111.
7 Cornelius Castoriadis, 'Done and to be done', in *Castoriadis Reader*, ed. and trans. D. Ames Curtis, Blackwell, 1997, pp. 400, 414, 397–8.

Chapter 6
1 François Chabot, 'La diffusion de la culture française dans le monde', *Cahiers Français* (Jan.–Feb.) (2009).
2 Theodor W. Adorno, 'Culture and administration', in *The Culture Industry: Selected Essays on Mass Culture by Theodor W. Adorno*, ed. J. M. Bernstein, Routledge, 1991, pp. 93, 98.
3 See ibid., pp. 93, 98, 100.
4 Joseph Brodsky, 'The child of civilization', in *Less Than One: Selected Essays*, Farrar Strauss & Giroux, 1987, p. 123.
5 Adorno, 'Culture and administration', p. 94.
6 See Theodor Adorno and Max Horkheimer, *Dialectic of Enlightenment*, Verso, 1979, pp. 216–17.
7 Adorno, 'Culture and administration', p. 103.
8 Hannah Arendt, *La crise de la culture*, Gallimard, 1968, pp. 266–7.
9 Milan Kundera, *The Art of the Novel*, from the Polish translation by Mark Bienczyk, Czytelnik, 2004, pp. 23–4.
10 Naomi Klein, *No Logo*, Flamingo, 2001, pp. 5, 25.
11 From private correspondence.